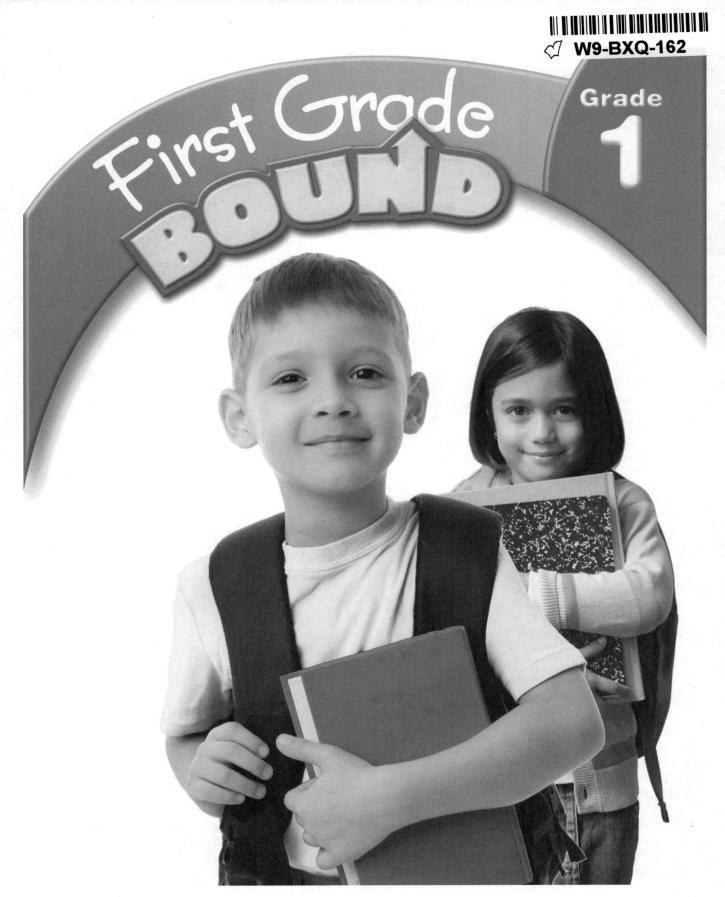

# First Grade BOUND

**Grade 1**

Thinking Kids™
An imprint of Carson-Dellosa Publishing LLC
P.O. Box 35665
Greensboro, NC 27425 USA

Thinking Kids™
An imprint of Carson-Dellosa Publishing LLC
P.O. Box 35665
Greensboro, NC 27425  USA

Printed in the USA • All rights reserved.          ISBN  978-1-4838-1285-4
03-032161151

# Table of Contents

## First Grade Bound: What Your Child Needs to Know

*First Grade Bound* is designed for the child who is entering first grade. It starts out by reviewing skills your child may have learned in kindergarten and gradually advances on to skills he or she will likely learn in first grade. Reviewing and practicing these important skills will ensure greater understanding and an advantage for the grade ahead.

This workbook addresses important language arts, math, reading, and basic skills your child needs to know to succeed in the classroom and beyond.

This guide provides background information about the skills and subject areas that are important for success in the coming school year. Tips are provided for helping your child develop in each curricular area.

## Basic Skills

During first grade, your child will be asked to demonstrate an understanding of basic concepts and commands. Activities in this book will help your child work with opposites, same and different, matching, and classifying items into categories. Your child will also be encouraged to use critical thinking skills to help solve word puzzles and mazes. Help your child explore basic skills by providing real-world experiences that encourage thinking and awareness.

- Classifying
  Organizing objects into categories can be done in many ways. For example, have your child group a set of objects by color, size, pattern, purpose, or other attribute.

- Critical Thinking
  Young children love riddles, jokes, and tongue twisters. Use these word games to develop your child's thinking skills. Critical thinking can be encouraged in many ways. Try asking your child to create a new ending to a common story or have him or her be the "teacher" and ask you questions about a story you read together.

- Compare and Contrast
  Help foster your child's ability to observe similarities and differences among objects. Begin with obvious similarities and differences in color, size, and shape and advance to more subtle similarities and differences in pattern, texture, purpose, etc.

## Reading and Language Arts

Reading

Teach reading with books that fit your child's ability and interests, using a variety of books. Before asking your child to read a book independently, activate your child's prior knowledge of the book's subject. Then, read the book aloud and discuss the story elements. For example, discuss the stages of a butterfly's life cycle and what caterpillars eat before reading Eric Carle's *The Very Hungry Caterpillar*. Provide books that your child can read independently the first time, while also reading books aloud that are at a higher level than your child's independent reading level.

- Word Recognition
  When encountering a new word, encourage your child to use three different cues: think about the context (meaning), analyze the sense of the sentence (syntax), and/or sound the word out phonetically. After reading a book, make flash cards of words that your child needs to practice. Maintain a word bank of words that your child is learning. Keep a separate bank of learned words to be reviewed periodically.

- Phonics
  Look for opportunities to teach the following skills in context: beginning, middle, and ending sounds; blends and digraphs, like **tr**ain or **sh**ip; rhyming words; and vowel sound families. Make charts to hang around the room for each vowel sound, and add words as your child encounters them in the books he or she reads. He or she will also study syllables and how to recognize the number of syllables when words are spoken aloud.

- Reading Comprehension
  Read to and with your child every day. Build a love of reading through positive experiences with books. A child who loves reading will be a more successful reader. Read a variety of books aloud, and let your child choose books that interest him or her to read independently.

The goal of reading is to acquire meaning from text. After reading a book, ask your child a variety of questions to test comprehension, such as "Explain what the character meant by …" or "Make a timeline of events in the story." Ask questions related to context clues to test your child's comprehension of information that is not overtly given and must be inferred.

Language Skills
Language skills are often taught in the context of reading. Your child may be asked to apply knowledge gained from reading to the study of words, sentences, and texts. When reading aloud to your child, take the opportunity to point to individual words, sentences, and punctuation marks on the page and talk about them. This will give your child a deeper understanding of how language works.

- Vocabulary Development
  Have your child write stories, in his or her own words, to be used as his or her reading text. This low-risk writing experience builds proficiency with language, and it helps him or her make the connection between the spoken and written word. Because this writing is in your child's own words, he or she will feel successful in reading at a very early stage. That confidence will help him or her be a successful reader of other printed materials.

- Types of Words and Sentences
  This year, your child will learn to recognize the distinguishing features of a sentence, such as capitalization, commas, and ending punctuation to indicate statements and questions.
  Your child will build upon his or her knowledge of nouns, verbs, and adjectives by diving into proper nouns, pronouns, plural nouns, and present- and past-tense verbs. He or she will also study contractions, like **don't** or **I'm**; compound words, like **mailbox** or **backpack**; possessives; and common prefixes and word endings.

Writing
In first grade, your child's writing will progress into full paragraphs of complete thoughts and conclusions. He or she will write to tell stories and share information. Learning to write is a process developed much like learning to speak. Provide your child with modeling and reasons to write, and applaud his or her attempts. First, emphasize fluency

in your child's writing, then move toward accuracy. Emphasize one writing skill per writing piece so that your child will not be discouraged by negative feedback. Keep a folder of your child's writing. From time to time, encourage your child to improve an old story or look over the year's work to check for improvement.

Speaking and Listening
Good speaking and listening skills are essential to school success. By paying careful attention to what is being said, your child will not only learn more but will develop the skill of being a good conversationalist as well. Make sure to provide ample opportunities for your child to listen to songs, poetry, and stories.

## Math

To teach math to your first grader, use hands-on activities and concrete objects to explain new concepts. It is important that your child understand the concept underlying a problem and not just how to solve it. During his or her first-grade year, your child should learn the basic facts through 20 and work to memorize them. He or she should also learn to solve two-digit problems and column addition, which involves adding three or more numbers together in one problem. Also covered this year will be place value, ordinal numbers, fractions, measurement, telling time, identifying and counting money, and graphing information.

- Addition and Subtraction
  Your child will focus on adding and subtracting within 20. He or she will be able to solve word problems involving situations of adding to, taking from, putting together, or taking apart. You can help your child relate math skills to daily living activities by creating situations and encouraging him or her to solve the problems.

  Addition is the combining of sets into a new whole. Provide opportunities for your child to discover that by creating and combining meaningful sets, a new set is created. While an eventual goal is memorization, it is essential that your child understand the concept of the part-part-whole relationships of addition and subtraction. It is valuable to be able to visualize that the number 5 is the same as 4 and 1, 3 and 2, 1 and 4, and 2 and 3. Addition as a mathematical process takes on more meaning for your child if there is a need for it.

Use manipulatives to introduce subtraction in the context of stories that your child needs to solve. Working with manipulatives also helps your child grasp the relationship between addition and subtraction. Provide a variety of practice so your child will have a firm understanding of subtraction and its uses.

- Counting
  There is a difference between rote counting and understanding the meaning of counting. Help your child develop an understanding of numbers through a variety of concrete counting experiences. Have your child practice counting sets of actual objects, rearranging them, and counting again. Activities such as these will help develop your child's understanding of one-to-one correspondence.

  This year, your child will practice skip counting by tens and fives (5, 10, 15, 20 and 10, 20, 30, 40). This is early practice for multiplication, which your child will begin to learn in the second grade.

- Skip-Counting
  Help your child begin with any number and count forward and backward by ones, twos, fives, and tens. Encourage your child to count while clapping, jumping rope, or doing other rhythmic activities.

- Patterns
  Patterns form the basis of mathematics and enhance problem-solving skills. Teach your child to recognize a pattern by modeling rhythmic and visual patterns. Have your child look for the pattern that is repeated in the sequence, then join in the rhythm or have your child complete the visual pattern.

# Basic Skills

First grade is an exciting time for children and parents alike, but it can also be a big adjustment. You and your child will face new schedules, new experiences, and new expectations in the coming year, but just remember—you're in this journey together!

For many children, this is their first year of a full day of schooling. For those children who attended half-day kindergarten, going to school for longer hours can be challenging. Your child may be tired and cranky at the end of the day, but don't worry. Most children adjust easily after the first few weeks. You can help your child have an easier transition by making sure he or she gets to bed early enough at night and eats healthy meals during the day.

As you work through this book, encourage your child to complete as much of each activity as possible and offer guidance as needed. This will give your child the confidence he or she needs to succeed in first grade and beyond!

This Basic Skills section will cover important skills your child needs to know, including:
- Identifying colors
- Classifying
- Matching
- Following directions
- Critical thinking
- Riddles
- Early writing practice

Name _____

Arrange the numbers to print a word that is part of your body. Then color each part.

*brain* brown

1. a r n i b
   3 2 5 4 1

*knee* green

2. n e k e
   2 3 1 4

*stomach* yellow

3. m o t c a h s
   4 3 2 6 5 7 1

*heart* red

4. t a e h r
   5 3 2 1 4

*lungs* blue

5. s u l g n
   5 2 1 4 3

*bones* orange

6. s e b o n
   5 4 1 2 3

*windpipe* pink

7. d p i n w i e p
   4 5 6 3 1 2 8 7

*kidneys* purple

8. i k y e n d s
   2 1 6 5 4 3 7

# Traffic Signs and Signals

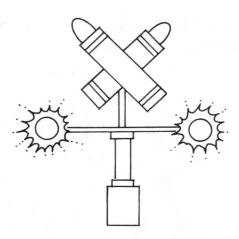

1. Color the STOP sign red.
2. Color the YIELD sign yellow.
3. Do NOT color the DO NOT ENTER sign.
4. Make the TRAFFIC LIGHT green.
5. Color the arrow on the ONE WAY sign black.
6. Color the WALK sign blue.

# Pyramiding Foods

Read the names of the foods in the Word Bank. Write the words on the lines under the correct food group.

**Word Bank:**
carrots  cherries
chicken  cheese
fish  ham  cake
lettuce  bagel  oranges
pears  rolls  beans
toast  pie  yogurt
candy bar  cottage cheese

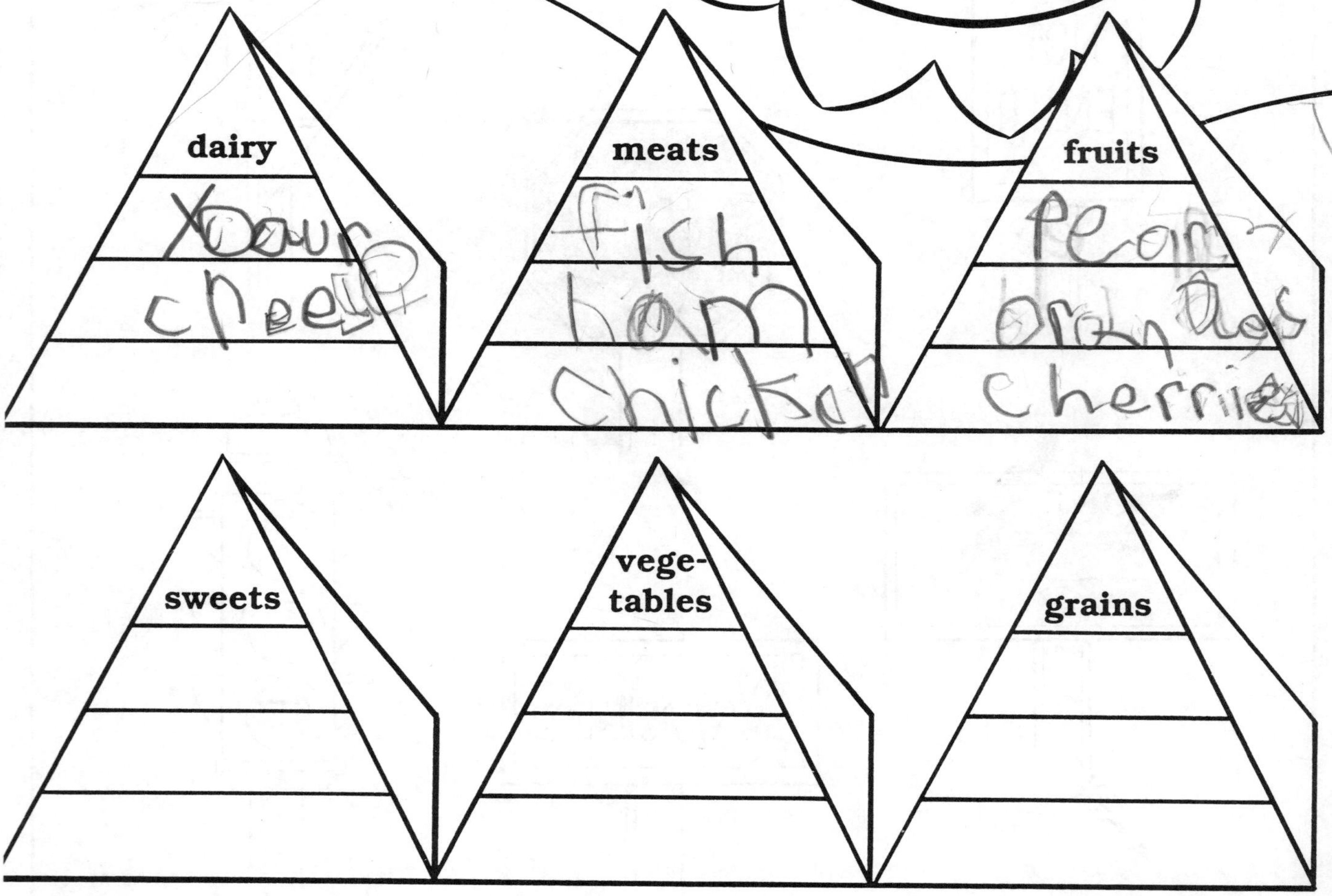

**dairy**
sour
cheese

**meats**
fish
ham
chicken

**fruits**
pears
oranges
cherries

**sweets**

**vege-tables**

**grains**

# Ocean Community

Many animals make their homes in an ocean community, but some of the animals in this picture do not belong.

Draw an **X** on the animals that do **not** belong.

# Pond Community

Many animals make their homes in a pond community, but some of the animals in this picture do not belong.

Draw an **X** on the animals that do **not** belong.

# Grassland Community

Many animals make their homes in a grassland community, but some of the animals in this picture do not belong.

Draw an **X** on the animals that do **not** belong.

# Forest Community

Many animals make their homes in a forest community, but some of the animals in this picture do not belong.

Draw an **X** on the animals that do **not** belong.

# Animals at Home

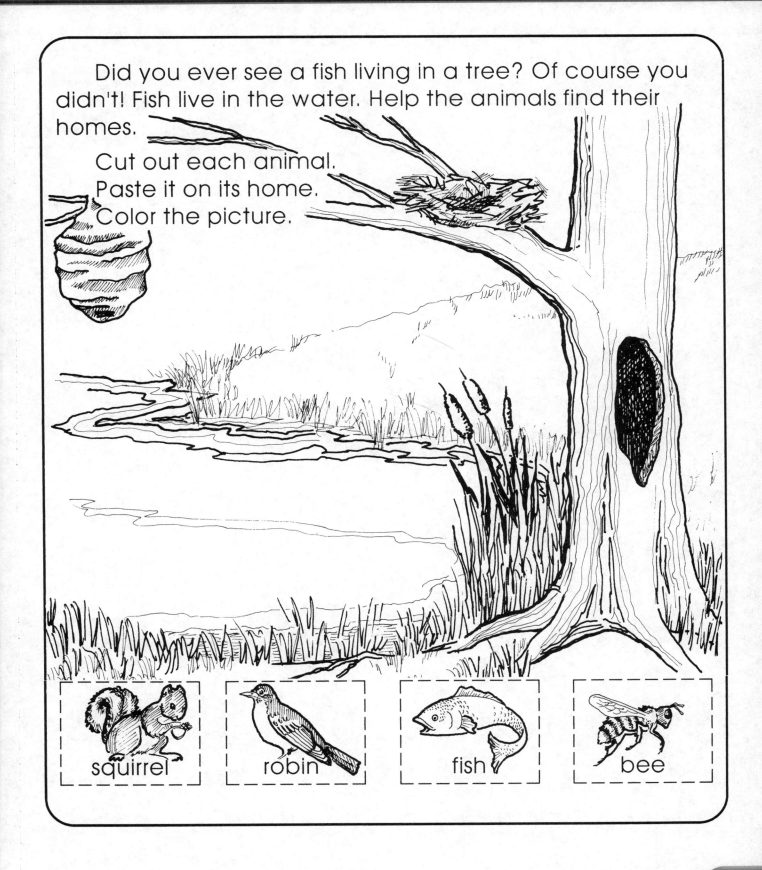

Did you ever see a fish living in a tree? Of course you didn't! Fish live in the water. Help the animals find their homes.

Cut out each animal.
Paste it on its home.
Color the picture.

squirrel    robin    fish    bee

# The Four Seasons

1. Cut out and paste the season words on the correct boxes below.

| Spring | Summer |

2. Color the clothes for:
   Fall – blue; Winter – red;
   Spring – green; Summer – yellow

| Fall | Winter |

# Pick a Pouch

Cut and paste each word on the correct kangaroo pouch. Then color one kangaroo green and the other your favorite color.

Animal Words

Color Words

| red | cat | dog | green |
| bear | purple | blue | fish |

# Cake Faces

Cut and paste the words where they belong.

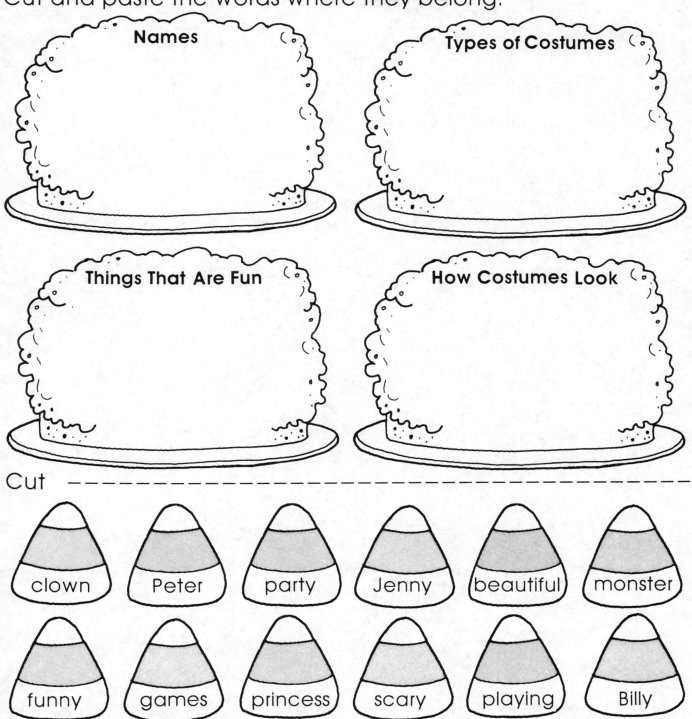

**Names**

**Types of Costumes**

**Things That Are Fun**

**How Costumes Look**

Cut ─────────────────────────

clown   Peter   party   Jenny   beautiful   monster

funny   games   princess   scary   playing   Billy

# What a Trick!

If the word names an animal, color the space **brown**.
If the word names something to eat, color the space **blue**.
If the word names something found in the sky, color the space **yellow**.
If the word names a piece of furniture, color the space **red**.
If the word names something you use in school, color the space **green**.

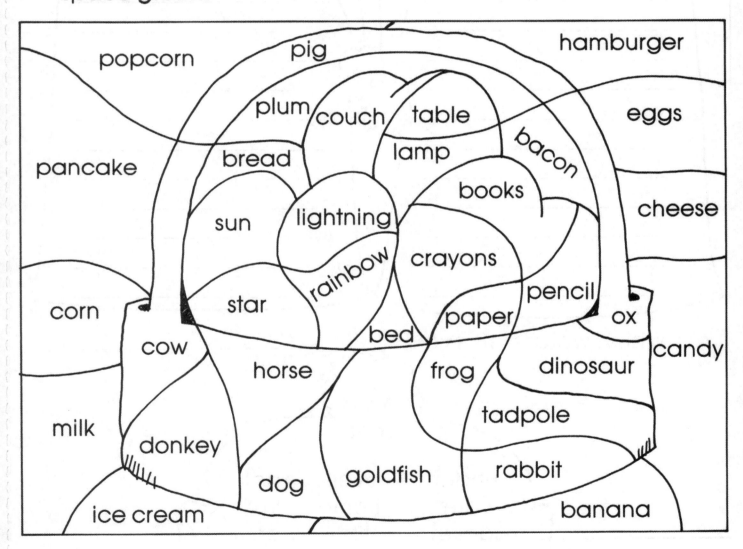

# "Cap" the Words

Read the headings on the caps. Write the words from the Word Bank on the correct cap.

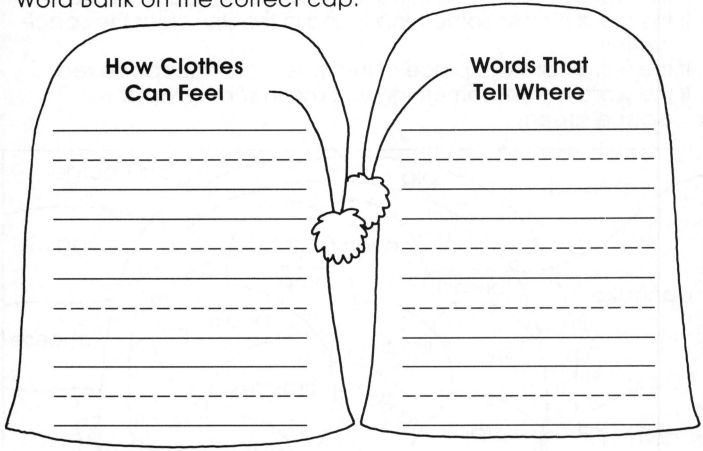

**How Clothes Can Feel**

**Words That Tell Where**

Which word is left over? _____

**Word Bank**

| | | |
|---|---|---|
| under | over | hot |
| warm | itchy | in |
| jacket | stiff | on |

# Where's My Baby?

Match the adult animal to the baby animal!

sheep

cat

hen

pig

dog

duck

cow

goose

goat

horse

chick

calf

gosling

kitten

piglet

duckling

kid

lamb

puppy

foal

# Leaf Shapes

All leaves are not the same. They have different shapes. There are four common shapes.

Draw a line to match the leaf with its shape.

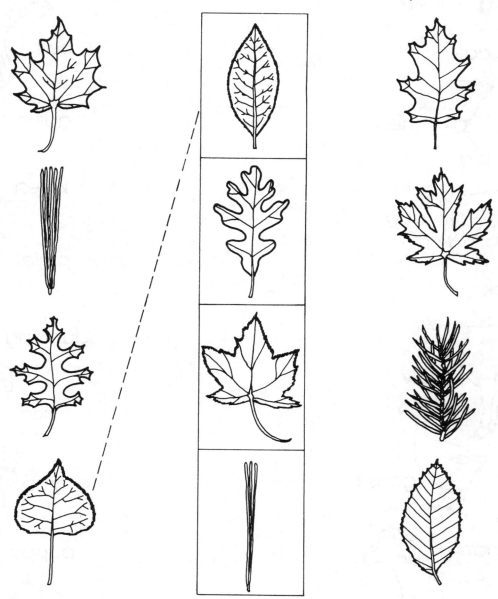

Find some leaves outside.
Try to match them to the shapes.

# I Slither and Crawl

Do the puzzle about reptiles.
Color only the reptiles.

## Across

2. A reptile's skin has _____ .

5. A _____ is a reptile with no legs.

## Down

1. A _____ is a reptile with a hard shell on its back.

3. Reptiles are _____ -blooded animals.

4. Baby reptiles hatch from _____ .

---

### Word Bank

| eggs | cold | scales | snake | turtle |

---

# A Reptile Riddle

Circle the animal that does not belong in the group. Print the letters beside the circled words in the spaces below to find the answer to the riddle.

### Birds
1. L   robin
   N   bluebird
   I   cow
   J   crow

### Insects
2. L   snake
   A   ladybug
   N   wasp
   T   bee

### Dogs
3. B   collie
   I   beagle
   S   shepherd
   L   ox

### Reptiles
4. R   snake
   I   horse
   G   turtle
   W   alligator

### Farm Animals
5. G   tiger
   K   pig
   O   cow
   Y   hen

### Jungle Animals
6. J   lion
   B   cheetah
   U   tiger
   A   rat

### Zoo Animals
7. M   bear
   O   giraffe
   T   dog
   F   zebra

### Ocean Animals
8. H   octopus
   T   whale
   K   shark
   O   camel

### Fish
9. R   raccoon
   I   perch
   V   catfish
   L   tuna

### Riddle
What do you call a sick crocodile?

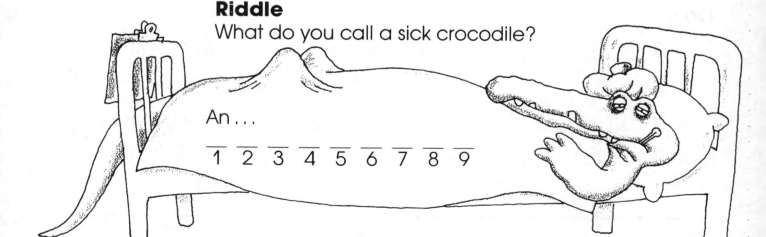

An . . .

___ ___ ___ ___ ___ ___ ___ ___ ___
1   2   3   4   5   6   7   8   9

# I'm Slippery and Cold

Do the puzzle about amphibians.
Color only the amphibians.

## Down

1. Amphibian babies usually hatch from _____.

2. Amphibians are _____ -blooded animals.

4. Amphibians often have smooth, moist _____ .

## Across

3. Amphibian babies breathe with either lungs or
_____ .

5. Amphibians live in the water and on_____ .

| Word Bank |
| --- |
| land    gills    skin    eggs    cold |

# From Mice to Whales

Do the puzzle about mammals.
Color only the mammals.

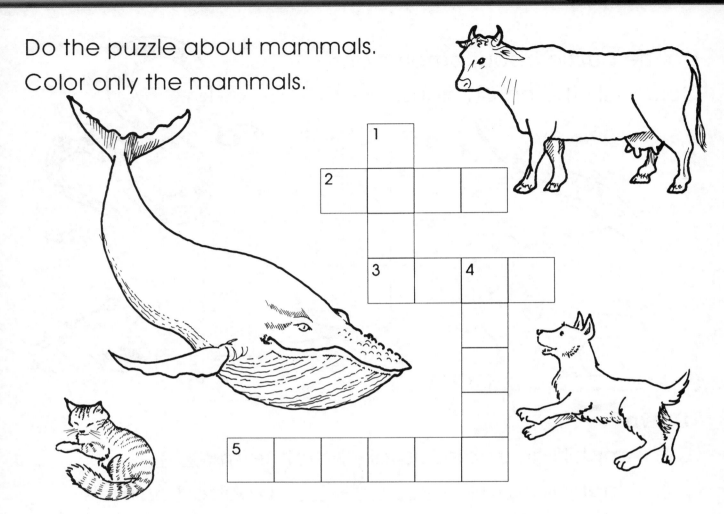

## Down

1. Mammals are _____ -blooded.
4. Mammals breathe with _____ .

## Across

2. A mammal's body is usually covered with _____ .
3. Mother mammals feed _____ to their babies.
5. Mammal's _____ are born alive.

| Word Bank |
| --- |
| hair    babies    lungs    milk    warm |

# Crawling with Insects

Do the puzzle about insects.

Color only the insects.

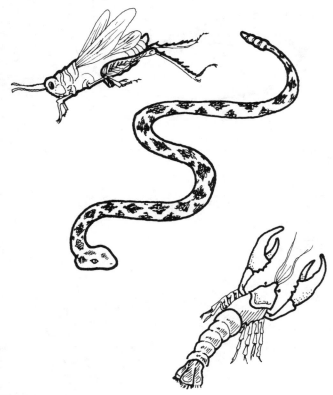

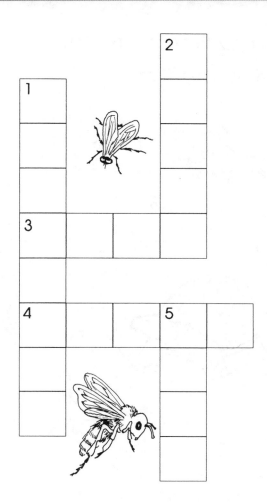

## Down

1. Insects have a hard outer _____ .
2. Many insects have two pairs of _____ .
5. Insects have simple and compound _____ .

## Across

3. Insects have three pairs of _____ .
4. Insects have _____ main body sections.

| Word Bank |
| --- |
| skeleton    legs    wings    three    eyes |

# Fish for Me

Do the puzzle about fish.
Color only the fish.

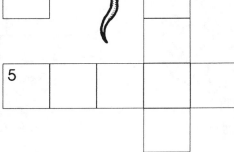

## Down

1. Fish have _____ , not legs.
3. A fish's body is often covered with _____ .

## Across

2. Fish breathe through _____ .
4. A fish is a _____ -blooded animal.
5. Fish live in the sea and fresh _____ .

| Word Bank |
| --- |
| water     scales     cold     fins     gills |

# Special People

Use the code to name the special people below.

| A | C | D | E | F | G | H | I | L | M | O | P | R | T |
|---|---|---|---|---|---|---|---|---|---|---|---|---|---|
| 1 | 2 | 3 | 4 | 5 | 6 | 7 | 8 | 9 | 10 | 11 | 12 | 13 | 14 |

12  11  9  8  2  4

11  5  5  8  2  4  13

3  11  2  14  11  13

5  8  13  4

5  8  6  7  14  4  13

10  1  8  9

2  1  13  13  8  4  13

# My Teacher Helps Me Learn...

1. Circle the words from the Word Bank in the puzzle.
2. Then color the circled words green.
3. Last, write your teacher's name on the bottom line.

**Word Bank**

| spelling | science | writing | reading | music |
|----------|---------|---------|---------|-------|
| art | math | gym | social studies | |

| r | e | a | d | i | n | g | w | r | i | t | i | n | g |
|---|---|---|---|---|---|---|---|---|---|---|---|---|---|
| s | o | c | i | a | l | s | t | u | d | i | e | s | x |
| w | t | y | s | p | e | l | l | i | n | g | b | z | p |
| o | p | v | s | c | i | e | n | c | e | j | l | x | q |
| v | w | p | w | m | u | s | i | c | p | q | h | i | r |
| b | s | c | t | m | a | t | h | w | q | x | z | l | y |
| t | u | o | a | p | a | r | t | h | o | n | f | k | m |
| k | m | r | s | z | g | y | m | e | c | d | o | b | n |

My teacher's name is _____ .

# Firefighter Find

A firefighter uses many things in his or her job.

Find the words from the Word Bank in the burning house below.

| Word Bank | | | |
|---|---|---|---|
| boots | hat | oxygen mask | gloves |
| ax | hose | fire engine | ladder |

```
o  f  h  p  x  f
x  w  r  n  t  i
y  h  o  s  e  r
g  s  c  l  g  e
e  c  v  a  i  e
n  e  a  d  v  n
m  f  n  d  a  g
a  m  t  e  f  i
s  a  s  r  b  n
k  x  h  a  t  e
b  o  o  t  s  l
g  l  o  v  e  s
```

# Scrambled Continents

Unscramble the words below to spell the continents correctly. Remember to cross out the letters you use. Put in capitals where needed. Use the word bank to help you.

1. rtonh miecara __ __ __ __ __  __ __ __ __ __ __

2. cfiara        __ __ __ __ __ __

3. eropeu        __ __ __ __ __ __

4. uhots ecaamir __ __ __ __ __  __ __ __ __ __ __

5. saia          __ __ __ __

6. tnrtaiacac     __ __ __ __ __ __ __ __ __ __

7. asurilaat      __ __ __ __ __ __ __ __ __

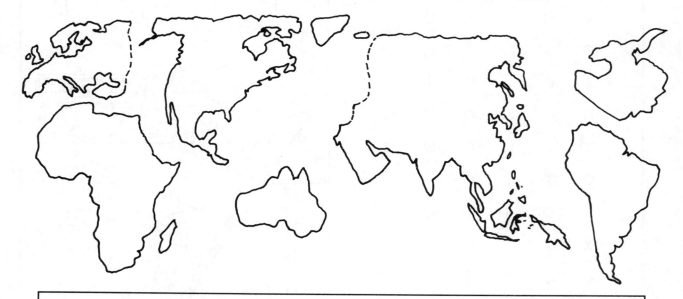

| Africa | Australia | North America | Antarctica |
|---|---|---|---|
| Asia | Europe | South America | |

# Alpha-bear-tical Antics

Follow the directions to answer the riddle below. In each paw, print the letter that comes...

1. Between H and J

6. Before S

2. After G

7. After K

3. Before N

8. Before B

4. After A

9. Between D and F

5. Between S and U

Now answer the riddle by writing the letter from each paw print in the space above the same number.

### *Riddle*

What famous lady bear was the first to fly across the Atlantic Ocean?

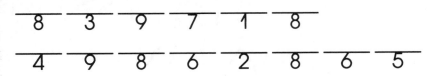

___ ___ ___ ___ ___ ___
8   3   9   7   1   8

___ ___ ___ ___ ___ ___ ___
4   9   8   6   2   8   6   5

# Plant Parts

A plant has many parts. Each part has a special job.

**Word Bank**    roots        stem
                 flower       leaf

Label the parts of the plant.

_____
– – – – – – – – – – – – – – – – –
_____
_____
– – – – – – – – – – – – – –
_____
_____
– – – – – – – – – – – – –
_____
– – – – – – – – – – – – – –
_____

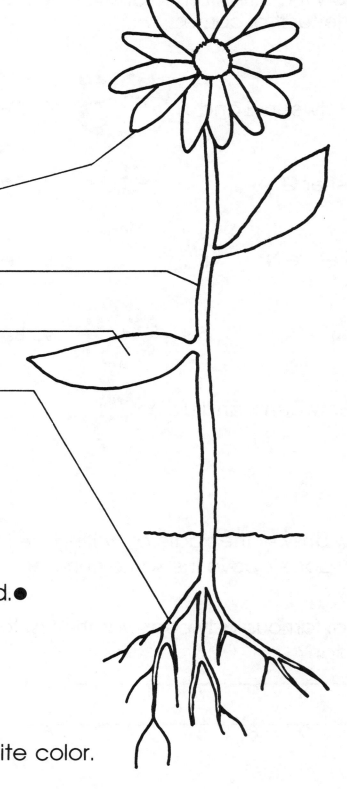

Draw a line from the plant part to its job.

I make the seeds. ●
I make food for the plant. ●
I take water from the roots to the leaves. ●
I hold the plant in the ground. ●

Color the roots red.
Color the stem yellow.
Color the leaves green.
Color the flower your favorite color.

# Feathered Friends

Name the parts of the bird.

_____

_____

_____

_____

Read the riddle. Name each bird part.

I keep a bird warm and dry. What am I? _____

I help a bird stand or swim. What am I? _____

I help a bird eat. What am I? _____

I make a bird fly high in the sky. What am I? _____

| **Word Bank** | | | |
|---|---|---|---|
| feathers | feet | bill | wings |

# "Hatch" Something Up

Many animals are hatched from eggs.

Read the clues. Then use the Word Bank to write the name of the correct animal on each egg.

I am a reptile.
I have big, sharp teeth.
I live near a river.

I live most of my life in water.
I eat tadpoles and water insects.
I can pull myself inside my shell.

I have feathers.
I have webbed feet.
I swim in a pond.
I quack with my bill.

I have feathers.
I live on a farm.
I have wings and make peeping
    sounds with my beak.

I live near water.
I eat insects.
I have a tail when I hatch,
    but I lose it as I grow.
I can leap up to six feet.

**Word Bank**

snake    frog

mud turtle    chick    duck

alligator

# When I Grow Up...

Draw a line to the correct answer.

1. I want to help sick people.

policeman

2. I want to fly a plane.

teacher

3. I want to help people learn.

artist

4. I want to be in movies.

pilot

5. I want to keep people safe.

doctor

6. I want to help sick animals.

actor

7. I want to paint pretty pictures.

vet

Read the following skills aloud. Ask your child to place a check mark in each box once he or she has mastered the first grade skill.

☐ I know the colors red, orange, yellow, green, blue, purple, pink, and brown.

☐ I can classify objects into groups.

☐ I can identify objects that don't belong with others in a group.

☐ I can match objects that go together.

☐ I can use critical thinking to solve word puzzles.

☐ I can use critical thinking to solve riddles.

## Now, try these fun learning activities!

Try these hands-on activities for enhancing your child's learning and development. Be sure to encourage speaking, listening, touching, and active movement.

- Play a silly game with your child. Take turns naming three things, such as **bread**, **butter**, and **pencil**. Ask your child to name which one does not belong and why.
- Discuss and list both good and bad manners. Teach appropriate manners at the dinner table, at a movie theater, and at a restaurant through role-playing.
- Have your child paint a rainbow. When the paint dries, ask your child to dictate a sentence about each color of the rainbow. Write each sentence on the arc of its color.

# Reading and Language Arts

Be positive and encouraging as your child encounters new academic skills. Don't worry if your child doesn't understand everything immediately. Instead, pay attention to what your child already knows well and then help him or her tackle new challenges. With enough practice, your child will begin to understand and master the concepts. That's why it's good to begin preparing for first grade now, so that he or she has every possible advantage!

As you continue to work through this book, explain the activities in terms your child understands, and encourage him or her to talk about the pictures and activities. These conversations will both strengthen your child's confidence and build important language skills.

This Reading and Language Arts section will cover important skills your child needs to know, including:

- Letter recognition
- ABC order
- Syllables
- Synonyms and antonyms
- Compound words
- Contractions
- Nouns, verbs, and adjectives
- Statements and questions

- Comprehension
- Following directions
- Critical thinking
- Drawing conclusions
- Main idea
- Rhyming
- Sequencing

# The Alphabet

_____ a line to connect the dots. Follow the letters of the alphabet.

# Letter Lift

Cut out the letter squares. Paste each square on the correct balloon.

Vowels

Consonants

o s m a q h d o r j x p
f g t i l b e n v u c k

# "Feast" Your Eyes on This!

Look at the picture. Find and circle the letters that are hidden in the picture that spell **Happy Thanksgiving**. Color the picture.

Name _____

Help the boat sail to the island! Color the fish:
**capital letters**—orange          **lower-case letters**—blue

# The Quail Trail

Read the words. Cut and paste them on the quails in alphabetical order.

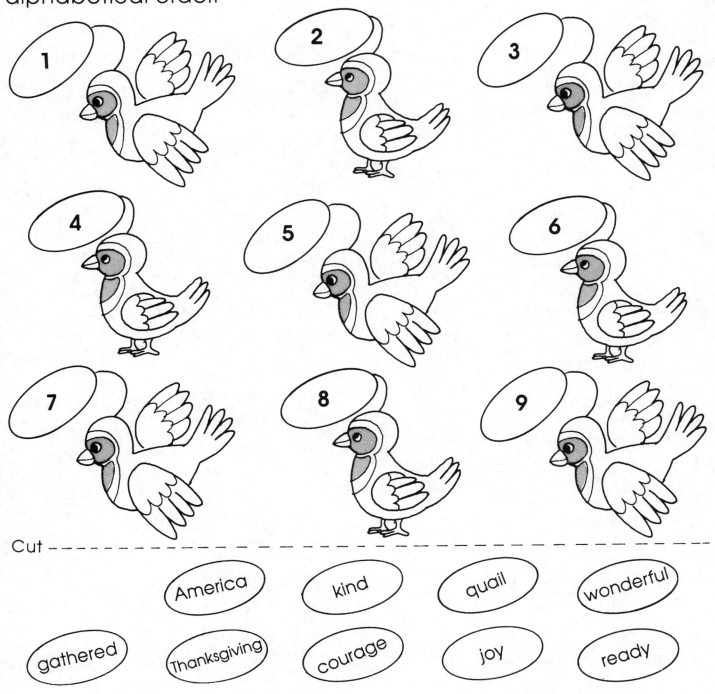

Cut - - - - - - - - - - - - - - - - - - - - - - - - - - - - - - - - - - - -

America      kind      quail      wonderful

gathered     Thanksgiving     courage     joy     ready

# Under-Cover Work

Color the pictures. Then cut them out and glue onto Ira's sleeping bag in ABC order.

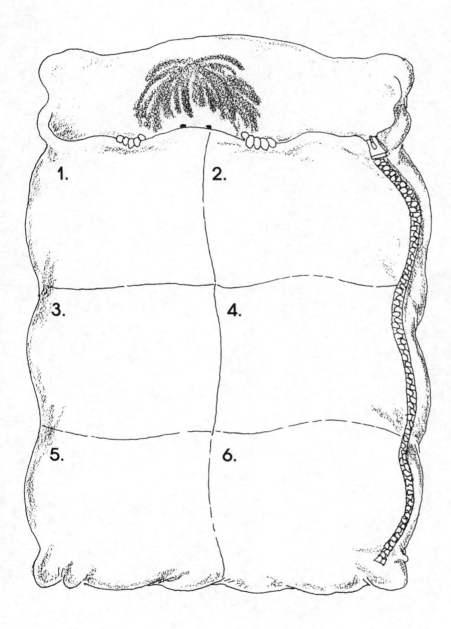

1.　　2.

3.　　4.

5.　　6.

dinner

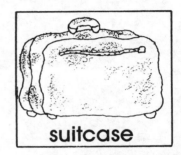

suitcase

bear

Reggie

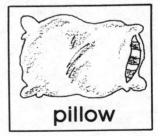

pillow

flashlight

# Morris Learns the Alphabet

To help Morris find his way to the candy store write the words from the Word Bank in ABC order.

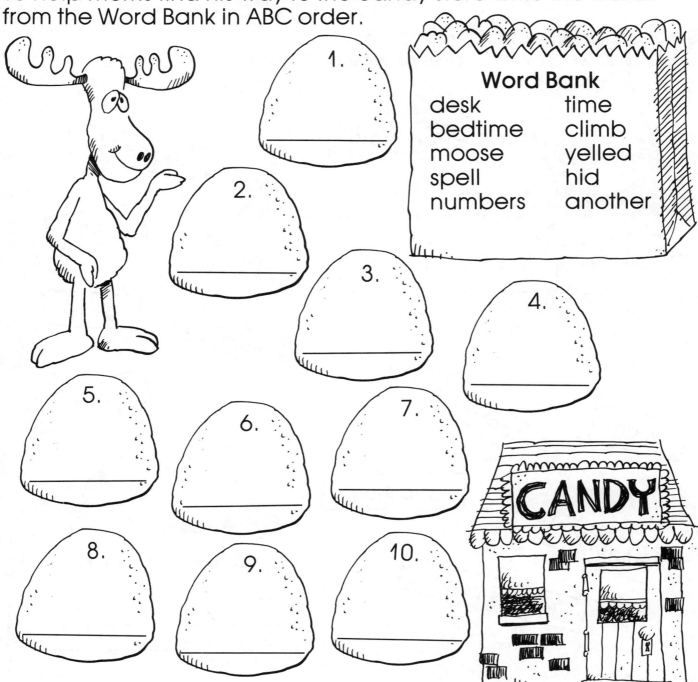

**Word Bank**

| | |
|---|---|
| desk | time |
| bedtime | climb |
| moose | yelled |
| spell | hid |
| numbers | another |

1.

2.

3.

4.

5.

6.

7.

8.

9.

10.

CANDY

# Ghosts and Spaceships

Write the words in ABC order on the correct picture.

Color space word boxes **red** and **blue**.
Color Halloween word boxes **orange** and **black**.

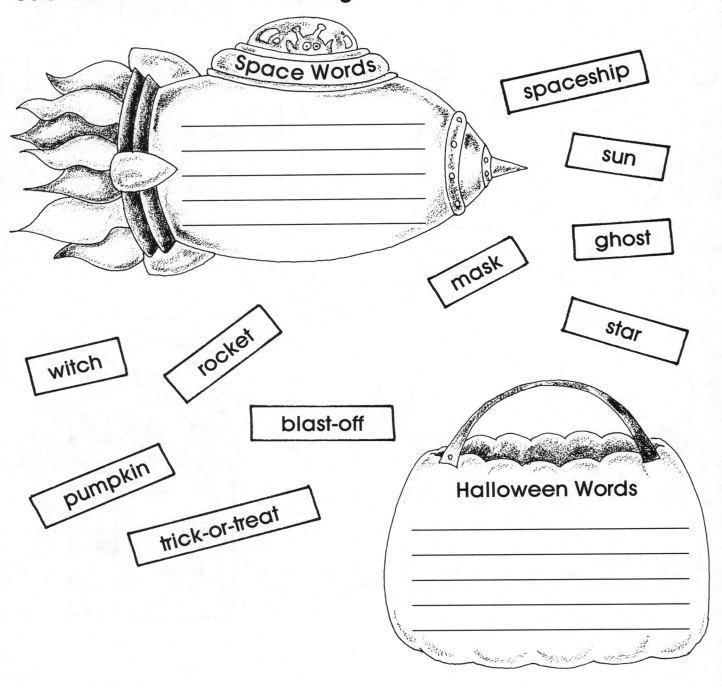

Space Words

spaceship

sun

ghost

mask

star

witch

rocket

blast-off

pumpkin

trick-or-treat

Halloween Words

First Grade Bound © Carson-Dellosa • CD-704634

# Take One or Two

Look at each picture on the cookies and read the word below it. Cut and paste each cookie on the correct jar to show how many syllables are in the word.

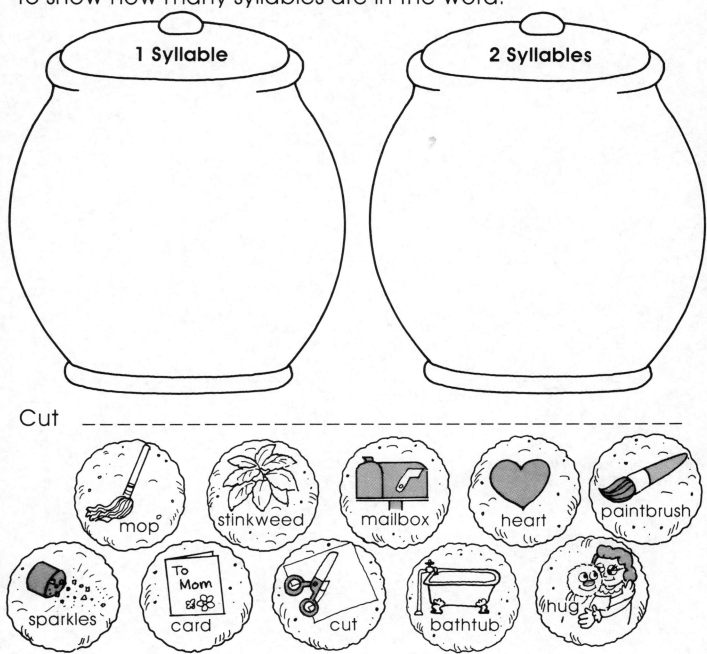

**1 Syllable**

**2 Syllables**

Cut _____

mop

stinkweed

mailbox

heart

paintbrush

sparkles

To Mom card

cut

bathtub

hug

# Two for the Dragon

Cut out the muffins. Glue the six muffins with two-syllable words on the dragon's tummy. Glue the rest in the center of another sheet of drawing paper. Then create and color your own dragon around these muffins.

king

poor

drawbridge

dragon

firewood

muncher

flour

bake

kingdom

villagers

bowl

muffin

## Bonus

Fill these muffins with your own two-syllable words.

# Similar Meanings

Read the words in the word box.  two words under each picture.

| | | | | | |
|---|---|---|---|---|---|
| rock | start | road | begin | street | stone |
| shut | sad | talk | unhappy | speak | closed |

# Select a Synonym

Read the words. ✎ the word that means almost the same as the first word.

| 1. big | cold | loud | large |
| 2. yell | shout | eat | jump |
| 3. small | good | thin | little |
| 4. smile | tall | grin | soft |
| 5. boat | talk | ship | hop |
| 6. look | see | fall | laugh |

First Grade Bound © Carson-Dellosa • CD-704634

# Attach an Antonym

Read the word on each person. Find the word above the hair that means the opposite and paste it on that head.

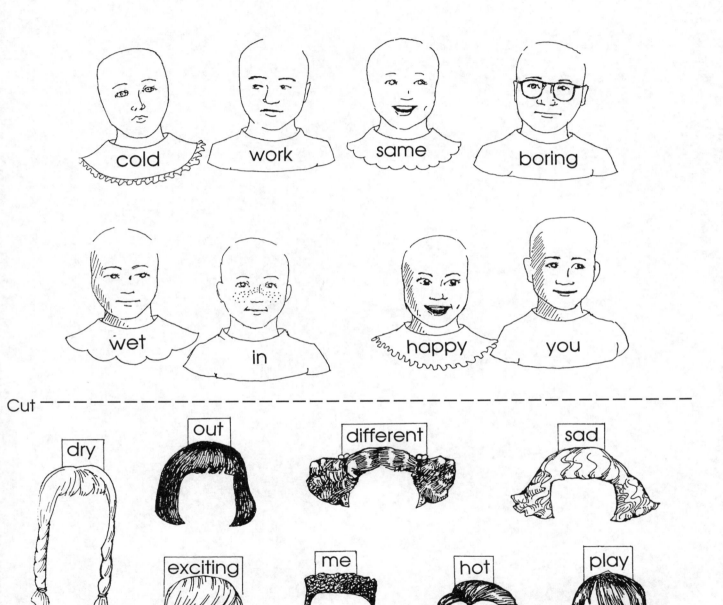

cold

work

same

boring

wet

in

happy

you

Cut — — — — — — — — — — — — — — — — — — — — — — — — — — — — — — — — — —

dry

out

different

sad

exciting

me

hot

play

# In or Out?

Read the words. Find a word in the Word Bank that means the opposite of each word given. Then write it on the line.

1. up        _____

2. in        _____

3. sad       _____

4. stop      _____

5. big       _____

6. on        _____

7. left       _____

8. here      _____

9. yes       _____

10. mother   _____

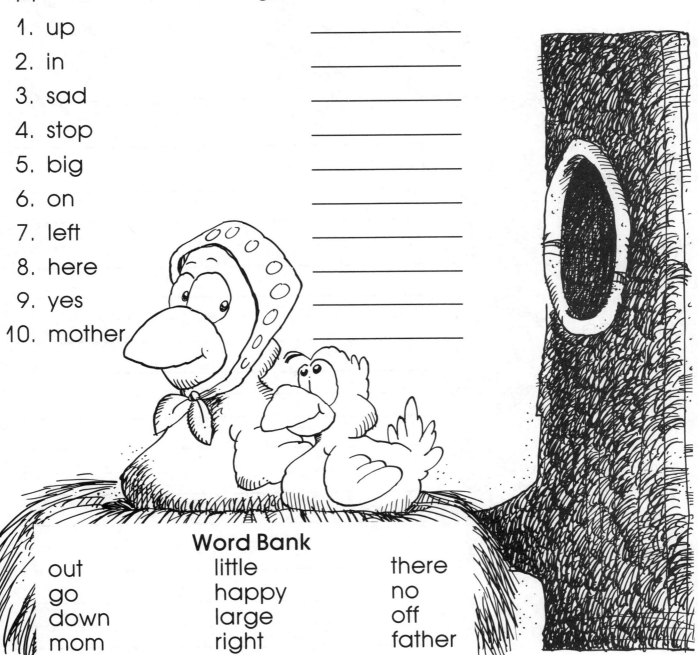

**Word Bank**

| | | |
|---|---|---|
| out | little | there |
| go | happy | no |
| down | large | off |
| mom | right | father |

Name _____

# Two Words in One

✏ the two words that make up each compound word below.

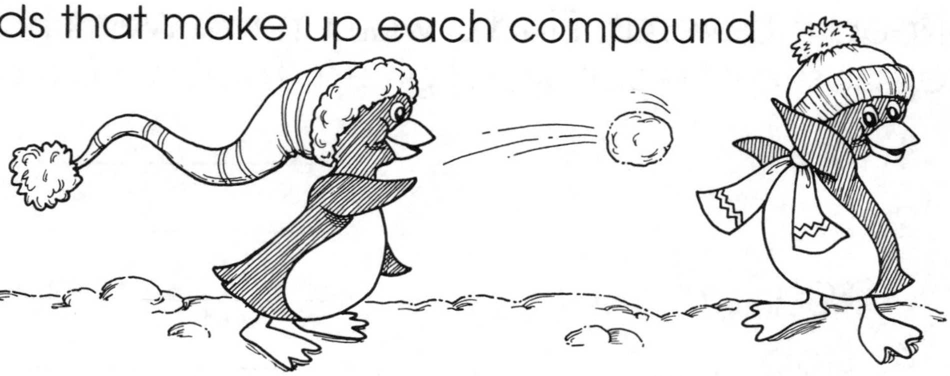

snowball

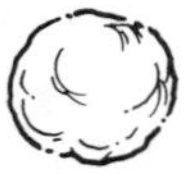

raincoat

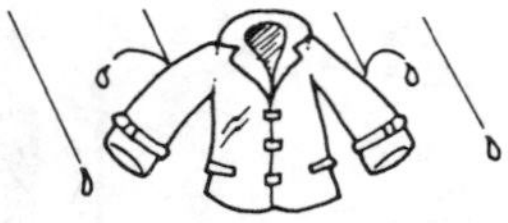

airplane

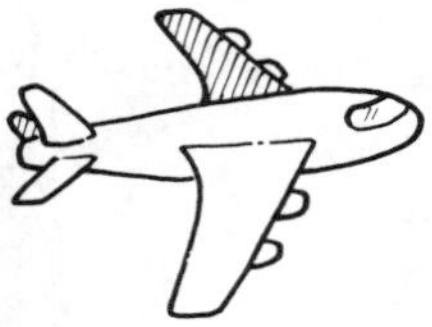

watermelon

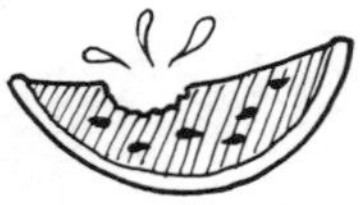

haircut

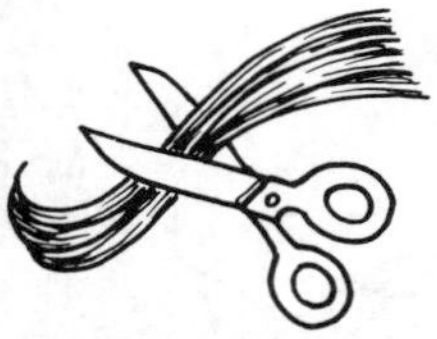

football

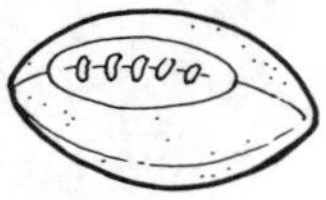

fingernail

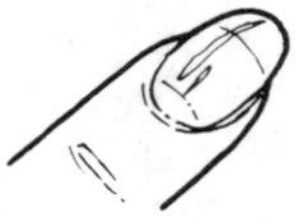

sunshine

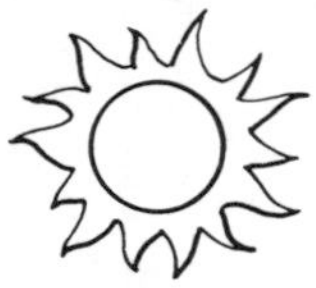

# It's Raining Meatballs

Draw a line from each word in List A to a word in List B to make a compound word. On another piece of paper, write the compound words and draw pictures of them.

**List A**

finger    basket    dog

pan    fish

rain    air    flower

snow

**List B**

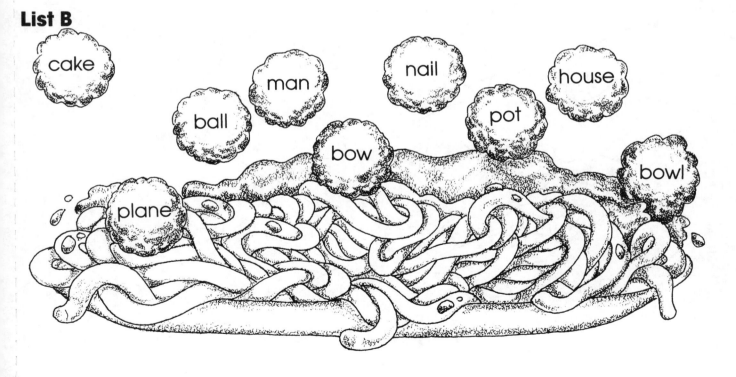

cake    nail    house

man    pot

ball    bow    bowl

plane

# "Compound"-ing the Cave's Echo

Read the words in the Word Bank. Find the two words that go together to make a compound word and write it on a bat.

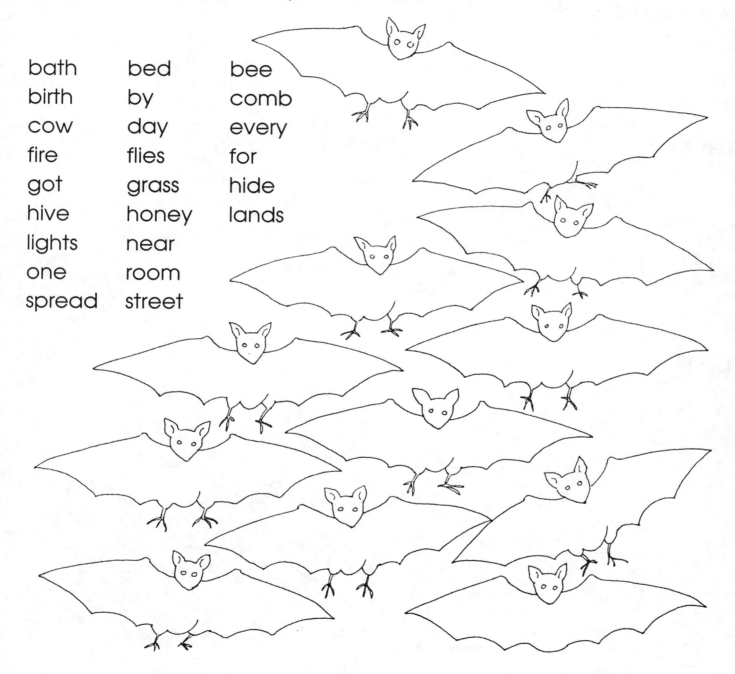

| | | |
|---|---|---|
| bath | bed | bee |
| birth | by | comb |
| cow | day | every |
| fire | flies | for |
| got | grass | hide |
| hive | honey | lands |
| lights | near | |
| one | room | |
| spread | street | |

# Let's Make a Snowman

✎ a line from each pair of words to the right contraction.

he is •                    • it's

it is •                    • she's

she is •                    • he's

they are •                    • you're

you are •                    • they're

we are •                    • I'm

I am •                    • we're

# Loppy Ears

A contraction is a short way to write two words. Choose a contraction from the big carrot and print it on the lines.

1. Leo _____ get his ears to stand up tall.

2. _____ not fun to be teased by the others.

3. "_____ not normal," thought Leo.

4. Doing ear exercises _____ help Leo.

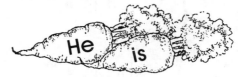

5. _____ go see the possum, he'll know what to do.

6. _____ my good friend.

7. The other bunnies _____ get their ears to flop down.

8. _____ all normal because we are loved.

I'm    We're    couldn't    can't    He's    didn't

I'll    It's

First Grade Bound © Carson-Dellosa • CD-704634

Name _____

# "Crumb"-y Contractions

Read the two words on the bread crumbs. Find the contraction in the Word Bank and write it on the bird.

we • are

that • is

I • would

I • will

she • is

they • are

she • would

let • us

we'd    she's
let's    I'll
I'd    we're

they're

that's

she'd

we • would

# Barnyard Nouns

A noun is a naming word.
A noun names a person, place or thing.

Find **two** nouns in each sentence below.
them.

| | |
|---|---|
| 1. The pig has a curly tail. |  |
| 2. The hen is sitting on her nest. |  |
| 3. A horse is in the barn. |  |
| 4. The goat has horns. |  |
| 5. The cow has a calf. |  |
| 6. The farmer is painting the fence. |  |

# Nouns on the Farm

Read the naming words below. ✏️ the correct naming word for each picture of a person, place or thing.

| | | |
|---|---|---|
| barn | farmer | pig |
| boy | tree | horse |
| girl | ducks | sun |

# Action Match

Find the action word in each sentence.  it.
____a line to match each sentence with the correct picture.

1. The dog barks.

2. The bird flies.

3. A fish swims.

4. One monkey swings.

5. A turtle crawls.

6. A boy talks.

First Grade Bound © Carson-Dellosa • CD-704634

# Circus Action

Find the verb in each sentence below and ✏ it.

1. The bear climbs a ladder.

2. Two tiny dogs dance.

3. A boy eats cotton candy.

4. A woman swings on a trapeze.

5. The clown falls down.

6. A tiger jumps through a ring.

# Falling Verbs

only the leaves that have verbs.

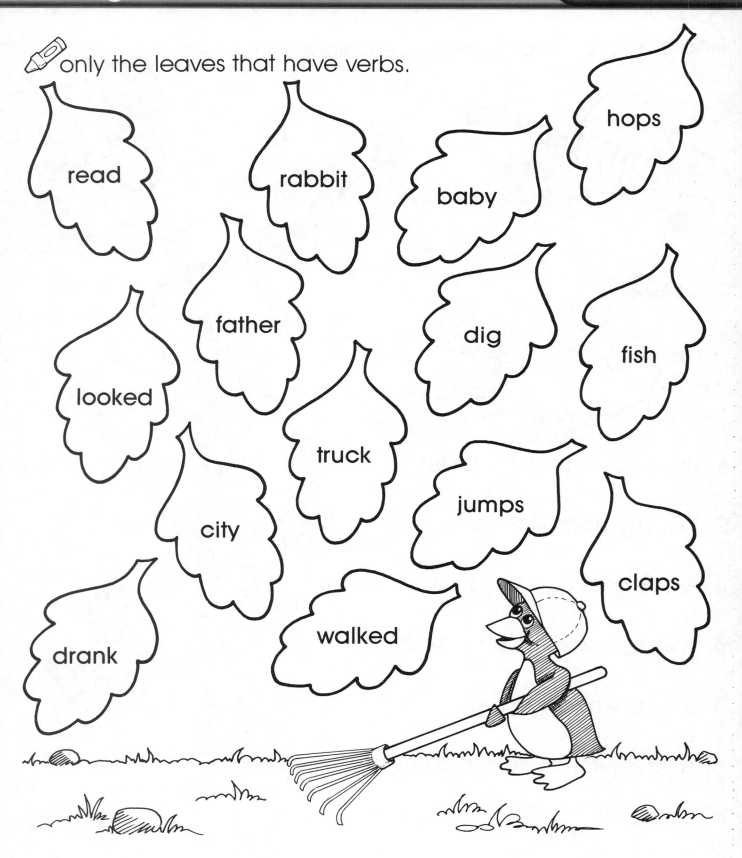

read

rabbit

hops

baby

father

dig

fish

looked

truck

jumps

city

claps

drank

walked

# How Did You Do That?

You use many parts of your body to do even the simplest activities.

Read each activity and write the body parts you would use to do that activity.

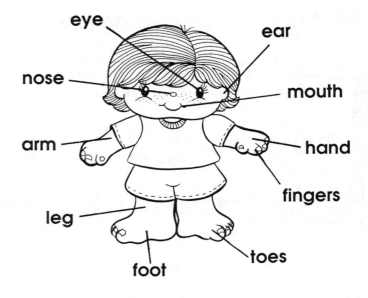

eye

ear

nose

mouth

arm

hand

fingers

leg

toes

foot

**Activities:**

1. read a book

_____

_____

2. talk to your friend on the phone

_____

3. put on your hat

_____

4. blow out the candles on a cake

_____

5. eat an ice-cream cone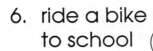

_____

6. ride a bike to school

_____

_____

# Animal Adjectives

✏️ a describing word in each sentence below.
Use the Word Bank to help you.

**Word Bank**

| big | bushy | three |
| round | green | six |

1. A _____ has a _____ tail.

2. A _____ has _____ legs.

3. The _____ will become a _____ frog.

4. A _____ has _____ teeth.

5. _____ _____ hang by their tails.

6. An _____ has _____ eyes.

only the fish with describing words.

# Corn Crackles

Here are some describing words:

| | | | | |
|---|---|---|---|---|
| sour | furry | sweet | tasty | crisp |
| tall | crunchy | cloudy | sad | soft |

Which four words do you think might best describe the cereal? them on the lines on the cereal box.

16 oz.

CORN CRACKLES

Surprise inside!

Puzzle on back!

# The Turtles Tell

> Some sentences tell something.
> Telling sentences begin with a capital letter.
> Telling sentences end with a period.

only the sentences that tell.

1. Two turtles sat on a log.

2. One turtle fell off.

3. Did you see him?

4. He swam away.

5. The water is cold.

6. Can you swim?

# All About Dinosaurs

the telling sentences below. Begin each sentence with a capital letter and end with a period.

1. dinosaurs lived long ago

_____

- - - - - - - - - - - - - - - - - - - -

2. many were very big

_____

- - - - - - - - - - - - - - - - - - - -

3. some dinosaurs ate plants

_____

- - - - - - - - - - - - - - - - - - - -

4. all the dinosaurs died out

_____

- - - - - - - - - - - - - - - - - - - -

5. no one is sure why

_____

- - - - - - - - - - - - - - - - - - - -

# State It!

Some sentences tell something. They are called statements. A statement begins with a capital letter and ends with a period.

✎ these statements correctly.

1. jenny planted a seed

_____

_ _ _ _ _ _ _ _ _ _ _ _ _ _ _ _ _ _ _

_____

2. she gave it water

_____

_ _ _ _ _ _ _ _ _ _ _ _ _ _ _ _ _ _ _

_____

3. it sat in the sunshine

_____

_ _ _ _ _ _ _ _ _ _ _ _ _ _ _ _ _ _ _

_____

4. the plant began to grow

_____

_ _ _ _ _ _ _ _ _ _ _ _ _ _ _ _ _ _ _

_____

5. leaves grew large

_____

_ _ _ _ _ _ _ _ _ _ _ _ _ _ _ _ _ _ _

_____

6. a flower opened

_____

_ _ _ _ _ _ _ _ _ _ _ _ _ _ _ _ _ _ _

_____

Name _____

# Did You Ask Me Something?

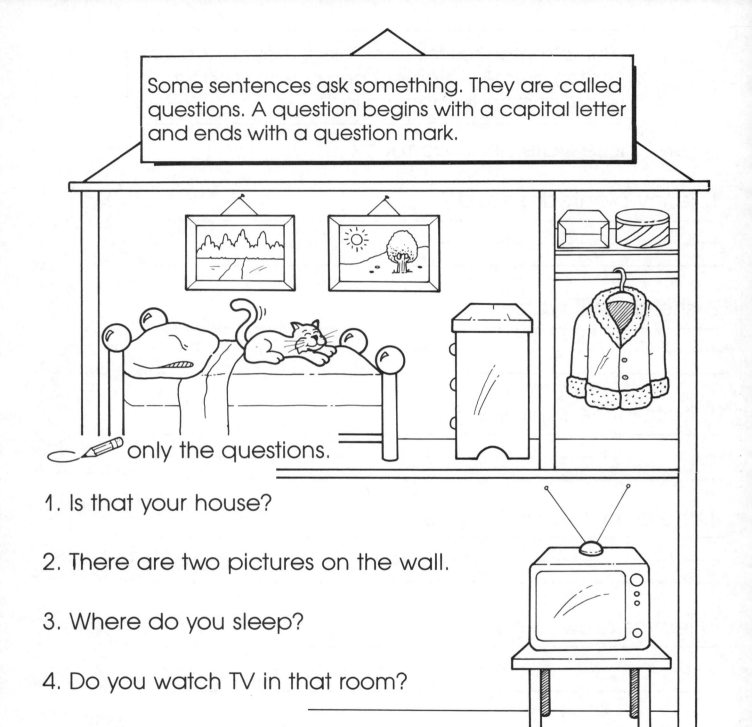

Some sentences ask something. They are called questions. A question begins with a capital letter and ends with a question mark.

only the questions.

1. Is that your house?

2. There are two pictures on the wall.

3. Where do you sleep?

4. Do you watch TV in that room?

5. Which coat is yours?

6. The kitten is asleep.

# Fishy Questions

the first word of each question below.
Remember to begin with a capital letter. End each
question with a question mark.

1. _____ that your boat___
   (is)

2. _____ you catch that fish___
   (did)

3. _____ much does it weigh___
   (how)

4. _____ you eat it___
   (will)

5. _____ you fish with worms___
   (did)

6. _____ the water cold___
   (is)

Name _____

A farm is a home for some animals. Horses, cows and pigs live on a farm. Sheep and chickens are farm animals, too. Many farm animals live in a big barn.

Which animals live on a farm?

ride    farm

_____

A _____ is a home for some animals.

Many farm animals live in a big

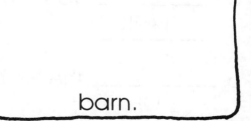

barn.

• Draw and color two farm animals.

# Pumpkin Patch Pick

Read. Cut and paste each picture where it belongs.

The pumpkin is in the wagon.

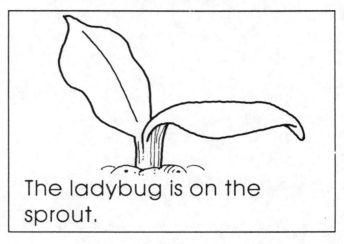

The ladybug is on the sprout.

The butterfly is on the flower.

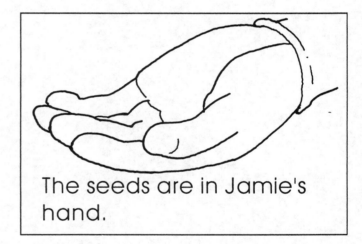

The seeds are in Jamie's hand.

Cut — — — — — — — — — — — — — — — — — — — — —

# My Pet

It is fun to have a pet. Dogs and cats are good pets. Birds and rabbits can be pets, too. Pets are good friends. They need care and love every day.

friends     fast
- - - - - - - - - - - -

Pets are good _____ .

Pets need care and   long.
                     love.

| dog | rabbit | cat | bird |
|-----|--------|-----|------|

# Mixed-up Colors

Did you know that all colors come from red, yellow or blue? They're the primary colors. Red and blue make purple. Blue and yellow make green. Yellow and red make orange. It is fun to mix paint to make new colors.

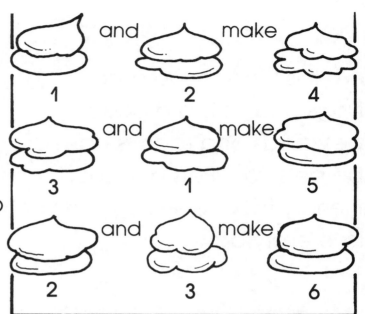

**Circle.**

Which three colors do you need to make all colors?

red        green        yellow        blue        pink

**Write.**

Red, yellow and blue are _____ colors.

orange        primary

**Match.**

Red and blue make                    orange.

Blue and yellow make                 purple.

Yellow and red make                  green.

Color the picture: **1** - red        **2** - yellow        **3** - blue

**4** - orange        **5** - purple        **6** - green

• Draw and color a picture using the **primary** colors.

# Just Hanging Around

Bats like to fly at night. They sleep in the daytime. A bat sleeps by hanging upside down. Most bats live in trees and caves. Have you ever seen a bat?

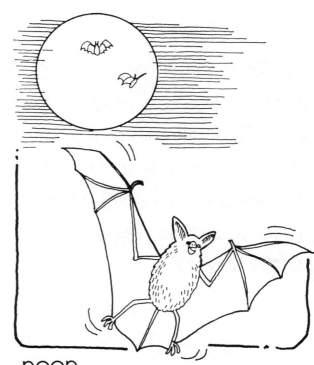

night        noon
_____

Bats like to fly at _____.

Bats sleep in the        room.
                        daytime.

How do bats sleep?

Most bats live in:
☐ trees
☐ caves
☐ floor

the bats black.

• Draw and color a cave with sleeping bats in it.

# Spinning Spiders

There are many kinds of spiders. Spiders have eight legs. They like to eat insects. Many spiders spin a web. The web is the spider's home. Have you ever seen a spider's web?

eight    four

_____

Spiders have _____ legs.

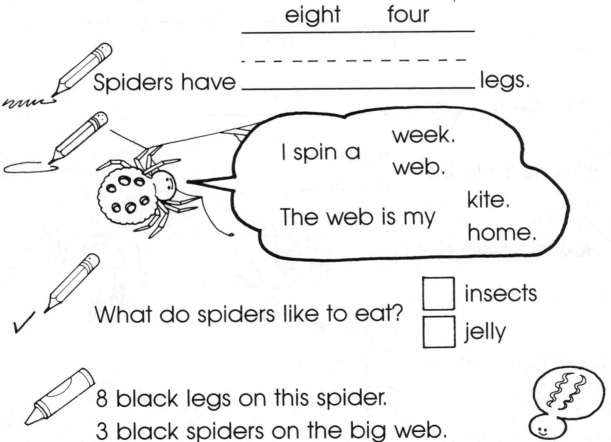

I spin a   week.
           web.

The web is my   kite.
                home.

What do spiders like to eat?   ☐ insects
                               ☐ jelly

8 black legs on this spider.
3 black spiders on the big web.

• Draw and color a spider and its web.

# Blooms and Birds

It is warm in the spring. Flowers begin to bloom. Trees have new  . Birds make their nests and lay eggs. Do you like to fly a kite in the spring?

warm    last

It is _____ in the spring.

What can you see in the spring?

What do birds do in the spring?

☐ Birds make nests.

☐ They lay eggs.

☐ They wash dishes.

• Draw and color a nest with four eggs in it.

# Fun in the Sun

Summer can be very hot. It is the time when kids are out of school. They have fun playing with friends, swimming to keep cool, and sometimes going on family picnics and vacations.

purple          hot

Summer can be very  _____ .

What happens in the summer?

☐  Kids are out of school.

☐  Skunks go on picnics.

☐  Kids play with friends.

What do you like to do in the summer?

_____

_____

_____

_____

• Draw and color a picture of your family on vacation.

# Autumn Leaves

The air gets cool in the autumn. Kids go back to school. Animals store food for the winter. Leaves turn red, yellow and orange. It is a pretty time of the year.

time      cool
_____
- - - - - - - - - -

The air gets _____ in the autumn.

What happens in the autumn?

☐ Kids go back to school.

☐ Animals store food.

☐ The air is very hot.

red          yellow          orange

• Draw and color an autumn tree.

# Winter Warm-ups

Winter can be cold and snowy. Animals stay near each other to keep warm. People wear coats, hats and . Kids can make a snowman. It is fun to play in the snow.

Winter can be:
- [ ] cold
- [ ] snowy
- [ ] purple

like    warm

We try to stay _____.

What do people wear in the winter?

gloves        hat        pan        coat

a black 🎩 on the ⛄.

• Draw and color a snowman.

# Our Planet Earth

Earth is a planet. It is the planet where we live. Earth has land and water. It gets light and heat from the sun. Earth has one moon. Many people think there is life on other planets. Earth is the only planet that we know has life. Do **you** think there is life on other planets?

**Unscramble.**

Earth is the _____ where we live.

l e t p n a
2 5 6 1 4 3

**Check.**

☐ I have land and water.
☐ I get light and heat from the sun.
☐ I have five moons.
☐ I have one moon.
☐ I am a planet.

**Circle.**

Earth is the only planet that we know has

stars.
life.

**Color.**

Draw one yellow moon in the picture.

• Draw and color a picture of Earth.

# Man on the Moon

Do you ever look at the moon at night? The moon travels around the Earth. It gets its light from the sun. Men have gone to the moon in spaceships. They have walked on the moon. They even came back with moon rocks to study. Would you like to walk on the moon?

**Circle.**
The moon travels around the    room.
                                                Earth.

**Write.**
The moon gets its light from the _____.
                                  Earth       sun

**Check.**
How did men go to the moon?    ☐ spaceships
                                           ☐ automobiles

**Circle.**
**Yes or No**

Men have walked on the moon.      **Yes**     **No**

**Circle.**
What did men bring back from the moon?    stars
                                                  rocks

**Color.**
Draw a red spaceship on the moon.

• Draw what you would do if you went to the moon.

# A Falling Star

Have you ever seen a falling star? Falling stars are not really stars. They are small pieces of rock. As falling stars fall, they get hot and burn. They look big because they give off so much light. That is why they are so bright in the night sky. Did you know that **meteor** is another name for a falling star?

**Circle.**
### Yes or No

| | | |
|---|---|---|
| A falling star is really a star. | Yes | No |
| Falling stars are pieces of rock. | Yes | No |
| Falling stars burn as they fall. | Yes | No |

**Check.**
Why does a falling star give off light?

☐ It gets hot and burns.
☐ It has a light bulb in it.

**Unscramble.**
Another name for a falling star is _____.

e r m o t e
2 6 1 5 3 4

**Color.**
Draw two yellow falling stars in the picture.

• Write a poem about a falling star.

# Feeling Fantastic!

People can have many feelings. They can be happy. They can be sad. Sometimes people can feel angry. Everyone has feelings.

 People can have many _____

five.

feelings.

| happy |
| angry |
| sad |

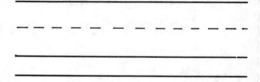

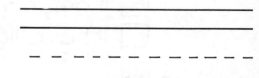

Make the faces look:

happy           sad           angry

- Draw and color a picture of how you feel.

# Fun with Friends

A friend is someone you like very much. Friends play together. Friends help each other, too. It is nice to have many friends.

_____ friend _____ from _____

A _____ is someone you like.

**Yes** or **No**

| | | |
|---|---|---|
| Friends play together. | Yes | No |
| Friends are cars. | Yes | No |
| Friends help each other. | Yes | No |

Which are friends?

• Draw and color a picture of you and your friends.

Name _____

A pilot is a person who can fly an airplane. A pilot went to a special school to learn to fly a plane. Some pilots fly planes for fun. Some pilots fly planes as their jobs. A pilot sits in a special part of the plane called the **cockpit**. Have you ever seen a pilot sitting in the cockpit of a plane?

**Write.**

The person who flies an airplane is a _____.

point    pilot

**Circle.**

**Yes or No**

| | | |
|---|---|---|
| A pilot went to a special school. | Yes | No |
| Some pilots fly just for fun. | Yes | No |
| A pilot drives a school bus. | Yes | No |
| Some pilots fly planes as their jobs. | Yes | No |

**Circle.**

Where does a pilot sit to fly an airplane?

cockpit

bench

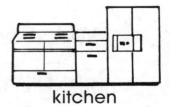
kitchen

**Color.**

Put green **X**'s on the pilots.

• Draw a picture of a cockpit with **you** as the pilot.

# On the Farm

Farmers have a very important job. They grow most of the food that we eat. Some farmers grow plants such as oats, corn and wheat. Some farmers raise animals for food. They sell milk from cows. They sell eggs from chickens. Many farmers use machines to help them do their work.

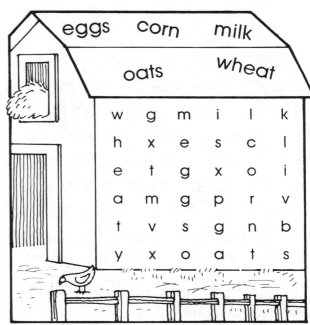

eggs  corn  milk

oats  wheat

| w | g | m | i | l | k |
| h | x | e | s | c | l |
| e | t | g | x | o | i |
| a | m | g | p | r | v |
| t | v | s | g | n | b |
| y | x | o | a | t | s |

**Circle.**

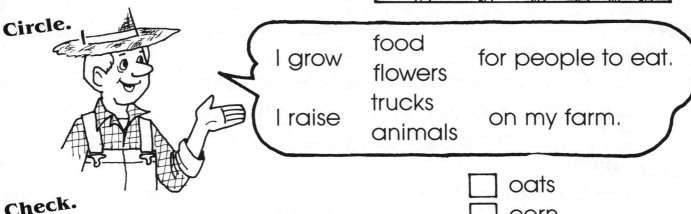

I grow  food / flowers  for people to eat.

I raise  trucks / animals  on my farm.

**Check.**
What plants do some farmers grow?

☐ oats
☐ corn
☐ steaks
☐ wheat

**Match.**
Which food comes from which animal?

milk        chickens
eggs        cows

Circle the words in the puzzle above.

• Draw a picture of three farm animals.

# We Care for You

Doctors help many people. They help sick people get well. They help healthy people stay well. People go to special schools to learn to be doctors. There are many kinds of doctors. There are doctors for children, eye doctors, ear doctors, bone doctors and heart doctors. Would you like to be a doctor?

1→bone

2↓eye

1→

2↓

3→

d o c t o r

4→

3→heart

4→ear

**Check.**

How does a doctor help people?

☐ A doctor helps sick people get well.

☐ A doctor helps people build houses.

☐ A doctor helps healthy people stay well.

**Unscramble.**

There are many kinds of _____. Some doctors are

c t o d o s r
3 4 2 1 5 7 6

just for _____.

h d n c l e r i
2 5 8 1 4 7 6 3

**Match.**

eye doctor
ear doctor
bone doctor
heart doctor

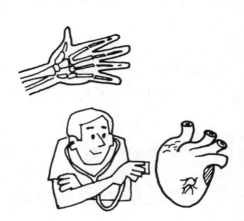

**Write.**

Fill in the puzzle.

• Write a list of three things you do to stay healthy.

# Animal Homes

Follow the directions below to finish the picture.

1. Draw a fish in the lake.

2. Draw a whale in the ocean.

3. Draw a dog beside the river.

4. Draw a goat on the mountain.

5. Draw a bird on the island.

6. Now color the picture.

# My Family

1. Color the  roof **brown**.

2. Color the  chimney **red**.

3. Color the bushes **green**.

4. Draw a picture of your family inside the house.

5. Write your address at the bottom of the page.

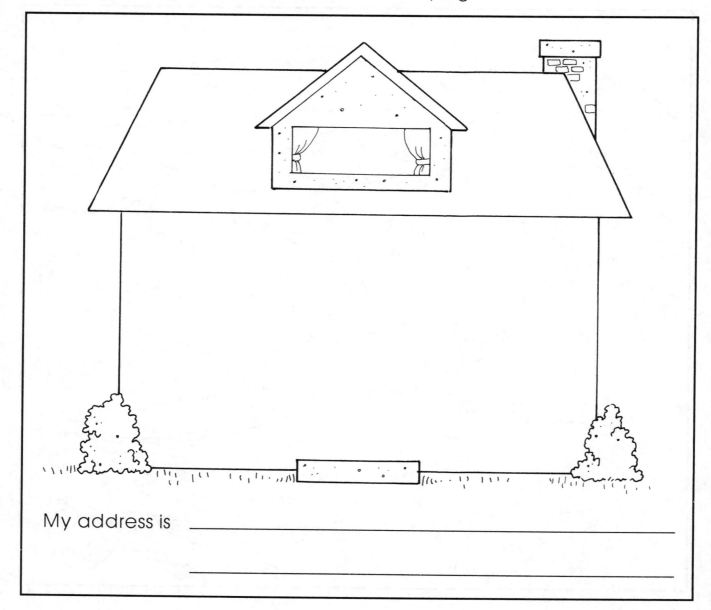

My address is _____

_____

# Native American Homes

1. Write **tepee** in box 1.

2. Write **adobe** in box 2.

3. Write **wigwam** in box 3.

4. Write **longhouse** in box 4.

5. Draw a sun on the tepee.

6. Color the longhouse **brown**.

7. Draw a door on the wigwam.

8. Draw small windows on the adobe.

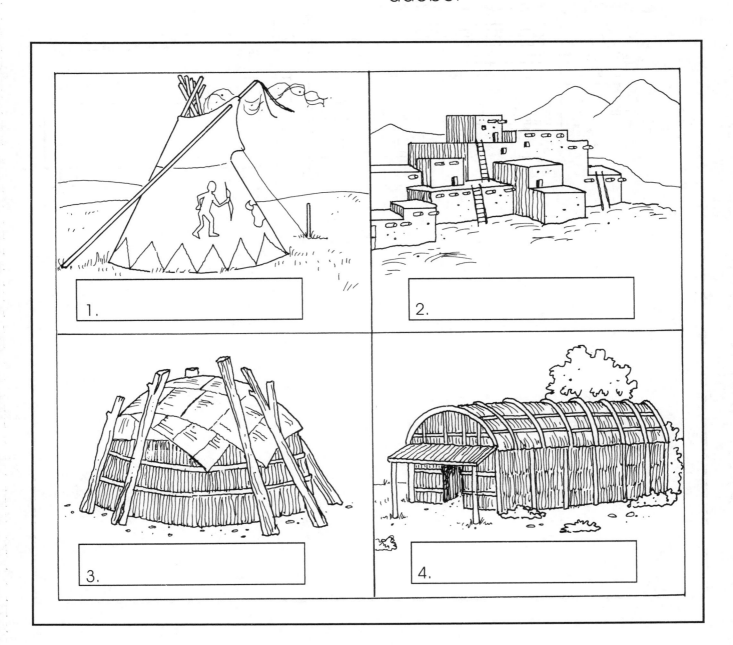

# Dressed and Ready

1. Draw a picture of you and a friend going to school.

2. Dress you and your friend correctly for the weather.

3. Write your school's name on the sign.

# Land Ho!

1. Draw a ◯ around the word **mountains**. Then color the mountains **black**.

2. Draw a ☐ around the word **hills**. Then color the hills **green**.

3. Draw a △ around the word **plains**. Then color the plains **brown**.

4. Put an **X** under the word **water**. Then color the water **blue**.

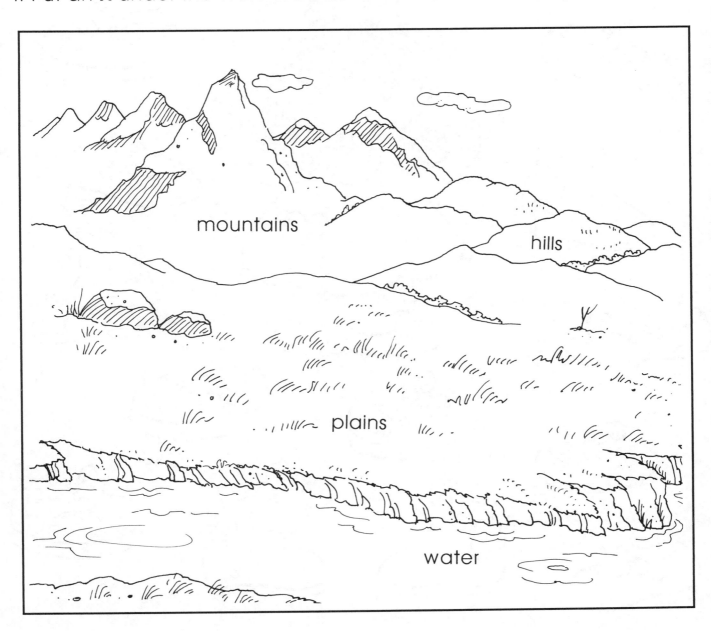

mountains

hills

plains

water

# Scrambled Shoes

Minnie needs new shoes. She tries on several pairs and decides on one pair. Oops! While trying on all of the shoes, she has scattered them all over. Now she can't find the other shoe of the pair she wants.

Help Minnie find her shoe. Using a different color for each pair of shoes, color each pair exactly the same. Then draw a circle around Minnie's missing shoe.

First Grade Bound © Carson-Dellosa • CD-704634

# Barbecue Mishap

Meg and her family are barbecuing hamburgers. A gust of wind blows the flames toward a tree. Oh no! The tree is on fire! A fire truck races to the fire.

Trace the different ways the firefighters can get to Meg's house.

How many different ways did you find? _____

Use a red crayon to trace the quickest way to Meg's house.

# Musician's Choice

Many different instruments are used to make music. Irene knows how to play several musical instruments.

Irene knows how to play these instruments.

Irene does not know how to play these instruments.

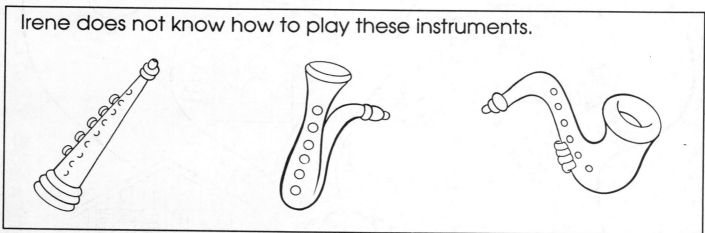

Draw a circle around the instruments Irene probably also knows how to play.

# Family Portraits

Families may be big or small. No matter how many people are in a family, each person is important to the others.

Cut out the pictures at the bottom of the page. Read the clues. Paste the pictures of the members of this family in the frame where they belong.

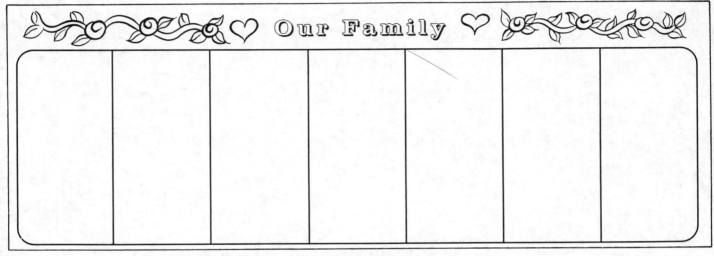

♡ Our Family ♡

- Grandfather is in the middle.
- The girl is on the right end.
- The boy is on the left end.
- Mother is between Grandmother and the boy.
- Father is beside the girl.
- The family cat is between Grandfather and Father.

# Playing Parts

Look at each picture. Find the title of the story that Grace is acting out in the Word Bank. Write it under the correct picture.

_____
_____
_____

_____
_____
_____

_____
_____
_____

_____
_____
_____

## Word Bank

| | |
|---|---|
| The Case of the Missing Cat | Cowboy Jake & the Roundup |
| Space Adventures | The Lost Treasure Chest |

# What Will They Do?

Read each sentence and question. 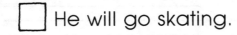 a ✓ in the box by the correct answer.  a picture to answer the question.

Draw.

The boy is putting on his skates.

What will he do?

☐ He will go swimming.

☐ He will go skating.

Draw.

The girl fills her glass with milk.

What will she do?

☐ She will drink the milk.

☐ She will drop the milk.

Draw.

The lady wrote a letter to her friend.

What will she do?

☐ She will throw the letter away.

☐ She will mail the letter.

Draw.

The kids gave Sally a birthday gift.

What will she do?

☐ She will open the gift.

☐ She will not open the gift.

# What's the Idea?

Read the sentence in each speech bubble. Underline the main idea.

My tummy hurts.

The mouse wants more to eat.
The mouse ate too much cheese.

My hat is blowing away.

It is a very windy day.
He doesn't want a hat.

I am seven years old today.

The cake is very big.
Today is her birthday.

I can't find my home.

The cat is lost.
The cat has a new home.

May I have more ice cream?

She likes cake best.
She likes ice cream a lot.

# Yes or No?

Read each sentence. Circle **yes** if the sentence tells about the picture. Circle **no** if it does not.

yes   no

The running shoe is very old.

yes   no

The tree has lost its leaves.

yes   no

The soup smells good.

yes   no

Two butterflies sit on flowers.

yes   no

The dog eats a new bone.

yes   no

The boy sees the plane.

yes   no

The snake is lying on a rock.

yes   no

The spider is spinning its web.

# Picture Pick

Look at each picture. Read the sentences. the correct letter in each ○ to tell the main idea.

○ 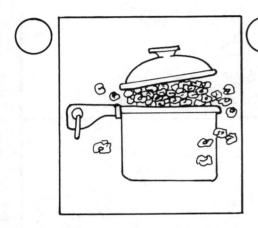  ○   ○

○   ○   ○

**A**- The eggs are ready to hatch.

**B**- It is a very windy day.

**C**- The old house is very spooky.

**D**- The popcorn popper is too full.

**E**- The girl thinks the music is too loud.

**F**- It is too warm for a snowman.

the pictures:
A — yellow
B — red
C — blue
D — green
E — orange
F — purple

# What About Bear?

Read each sentence. Circle **yes** if the sentence tells about the picture. Circle **no** if it does not.

yes    no

It is a very hot day.

yes    no

The hat is too small.

yes    no

The bear is afraid of the mouse.

yes    no

The bear washed three shirts.

yes    no

The circus is lots of fun.

yes    no

The bear has two mittens.

yes    no

The bear walks to school.

yes    no

The bear likes to cook.

Read the word on each mitten. Find the word on a snowball that rhymes with it. Cut and paste the snowball on the correct mitten. Color the mittens.

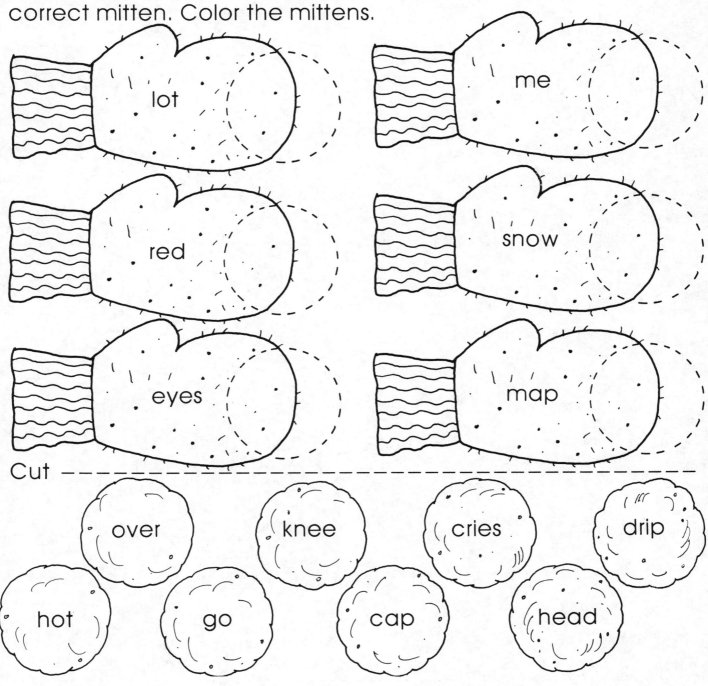

lot

me

red

snow

eyes

map

Cut - - - - - - - - - - - - - - - - - - - - - - - - - - - -

over

knee

cries

drip

hot

go

cap

head

# Strawberry Patch Match

Read the word on each strawberry. Find the word in the Word Bank that rhymes. Write it on the line.

sun _____

Sam _____

sky _____

day _____

bark _____

goat _____

kite _____

tea _____

flowers _____

cool _____

## Word Bank

| away | boat | high | fun |
|------|------|------|-----|
| might | park | tree | jam |
| | showers | school | |

# A Space Case!

Read the word on each spaceship. Find the words in the Word Bank that rhyme and write them on the line.

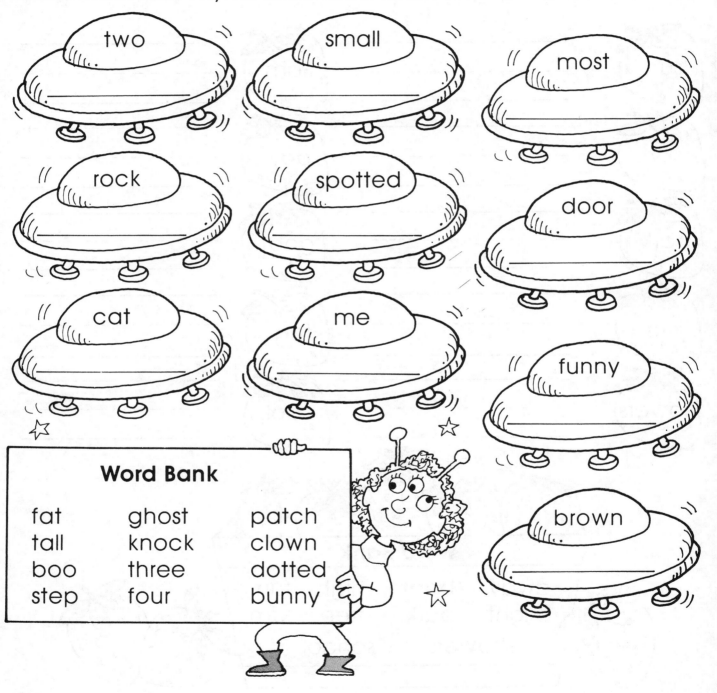

two

small

most

rock

spotted

door

cat

me

funny

brown

**Word Bank**

| | | |
|---|---|---|
| fat | ghost | patch |
| tall | knock | clown |
| boo | three | dotted |
| step | four | bunny |

126

# Carrot Crop

the four pictures. and the pictures in 1, 2, 3, 4 order.

# Fall Pick Up

Color the pictures. Cut and paste each picture in **1**, **2**, **3**, **4** order.

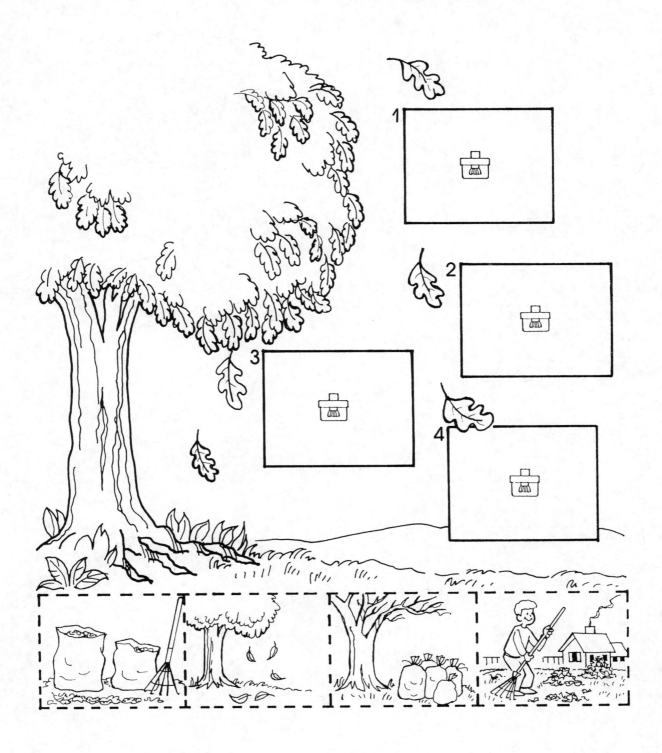

# It's Hard to Wait!

Write **1**, **2**, **3**, or **4** in the boot next to the picture to show the order it happened in the story. Then draw a line from the boot to the sentence that tells about that picture.

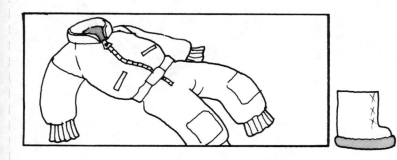    He has a new snowsuit.

   He made a snowball.

   He put on his new snowsuit, boots, hat and mittens.

   He wished and wished for snow.

# Home Rules

1. Number the pictures in the correct order.
2. Then color the pictures.

Keep your room clean.

Be helpful.

Take care of the yard.

# My Friend the Bear

Read each sentence. If it tells something that could really happen, color the real bear. If it tells something that is make-believe, color the toy bear.

**Real**     **Make-Believe**

1. A bear can live in a forest.

2. A bear can search in a store for a lost button.

3. A girl can sew a button on a pair of overalls.

4. A bear can talk to a little girl.

5. A toy bear can ride up an escalator by himself.

6. A toy bear can sit on a toy department shelf.

7. A little girl can save money in a piggy bank.

8. A toy bear and a little girl can be friends.

9. A toy bear can yank a button off a mattress.

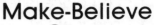

Read the following skills aloud. Ask your child to place a check mark in each box once he or she has mastered the first grade skill.

☐ I can identify upper- and lowercase letters.
☐ I can place letters and words in ABC order.
☐ I can identify words containing two or three syllables.
☐ I can form compound words and identify the two words that make them up.
☐ I can form and identify the contractions **it's**, **she's**, **he's**, **you're**, **they're**, **I'm**, **we're**, **can't**, **didn't**, **I'll**, **couldn't**, **we'd**, **let's**, **I'd**, **that's**, and **she'd**.
☐ I can identify nouns, verbs, and adjectives.
☐ I can identify statements and questions.
☐ I can place events in the correct sequence.
☐ I can answer questions about something I've read.
☐ I can follow directions.
☐ I can draw conclusions about what might happen next.
☐ I can determine the main idea of something I've read.
☐ I understand and can identify rhyming words.
☐ I can place text and pictures in sequential order.

## Now, try these fun learning activities!

Try these hands-on activities for enhancing your child's learning and development. Be sure to encourage speaking, listening, touching, and active movement.

- On a chart, label two columns **One Syllable** and **Two Syllables**. Have your child listen as you say some one- and two-syllable words. Tell your child to repeat each word and clap the number of syllables in it. Under your child's direction, list words in the appropriate column of the chart.
- Review nouns, adjectives, and verbs with your child. Have your child look in books he or she has read for 10 nouns, 10 adjectives, and 10 verbs. Have your child sort and label the categories and then write three sentences using some of the found words.
- Discuss the beginning, middle, and end of *Where the Wild Things Are* by Maurice Sendak. Have your child draw the sequence of events from the story in a comic strip format. Have him or her write simple dialogue in balloons as in comic strips.

# Math

As you help your child get ready for first grade, remember that your goal is to nurture excitement for learning. Skills are learned best if they are not turned into lessons. Introduce skills naturally in small doses, reinforcing from time to time through casual conversations and play. Here are some things to keep in mind when helping your first grader learn:

**Allow your child to learn by doing.** Hands-on activities help children take learning off the page and into their own hands. Learning becomes something fun, not just something that needs to be done. It also helps children apply skills and activities to real-world situations and helps them understand meaning in relation to the world around them.

**Read, read, read, read to your child!** Reading is one of the most important things you can do with your child. The more children read or are read to, the better they become at reading, which, in turn, makes it an enjoyable activity. Reading can enhance your child's social skills and open up new worlds!

**Envelop your child in language.** Describe, explain, and communicate at every opportunity, whether you are walking down the street, shopping at the grocery, or preparing dinner. Encourage conversation with your child to foster language and social development.

**Praise your child for asking questions.** Asking a question shows a high level of thinking and reasoning.

This Math section will cover important skills your child needs to know, including:

- Shapes
- Size words
- Patterns
- Number recognition
- Counting
- Skip counting

- Addition and subtraction
- Fractions
- Ordinal numbers
- Money
- Time
- Measurement

# Special Hearts for a Special Friend

Look at the picture carefully.

How many hearts were used to draw the cat? _____

Draw and color a picture of an animal using only heart shapes.

First Grade Bound © Carson-Dellosa • CD-704634

# Animal Action

Find the shapes and color the picture using the code.

○ red    □ blue    ▭ yellow

△ green    ◇ orange    ⬭ black

# Cabin to Capitol

Abraham Lincoln was the 16th president of the United States. He was born in a log cabin. Many people lived in log cabins at that time.

Look at this picture of a log cabin. How many of each of the different shapes can you find in the picture?

How many  's? _____     How many ⬭ 's? _____

How many ☐ 's? _____     Draw and color a door.

# Mask Make-Up

Masks have been made by people for many years. In some countries, the actors in plays wear masks. Masks can be made from wood, metal, paper, cloth, or even foil. They can be painted with a design or a face. Color the mask by using the color code.

○ **red**  ☐ **orange**  △ **yellow**  ▭ **blue**

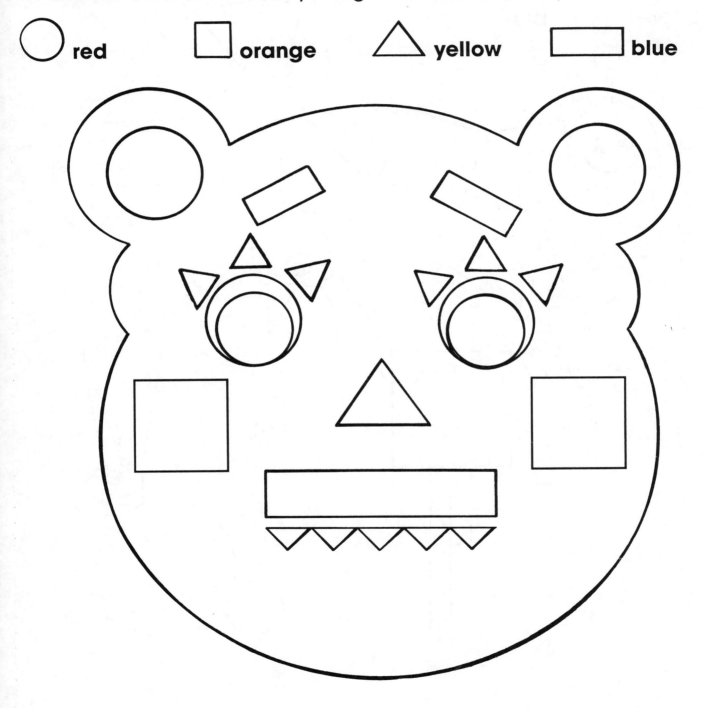

# Animal Shapes

Color:

squares —— green
rectangles —— yellow
circles —— red
triangles —— blue

# Confection Perfection

Cut out the pictures of the candy at the bottom of the page. Paste the pictures to correctly continue the pattern in each row.

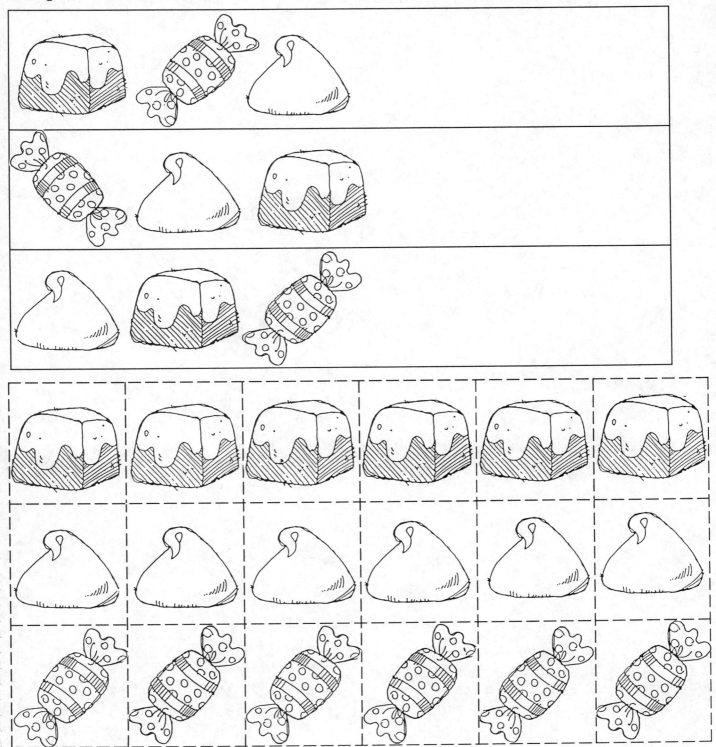

# Roaring Roller-Coaster Rides

Cut out the roller coaster cars at the bottom of the page. Paste them to correctly continue the pattern on each track.

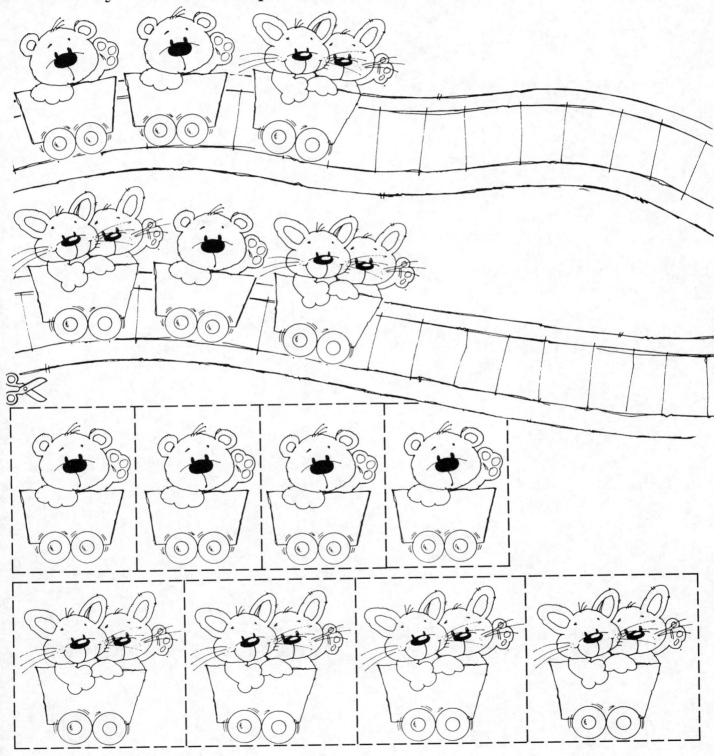

# Strawberry Stack-Up

Farmers grow ripe, red strawberries for everyone to eat. Before taking the strawberries to the stores, the farmers put them in small baskets.

Look at the pattern of the baskets in each row. Draw the correct number of strawberries in the baskets to continue each pattern.

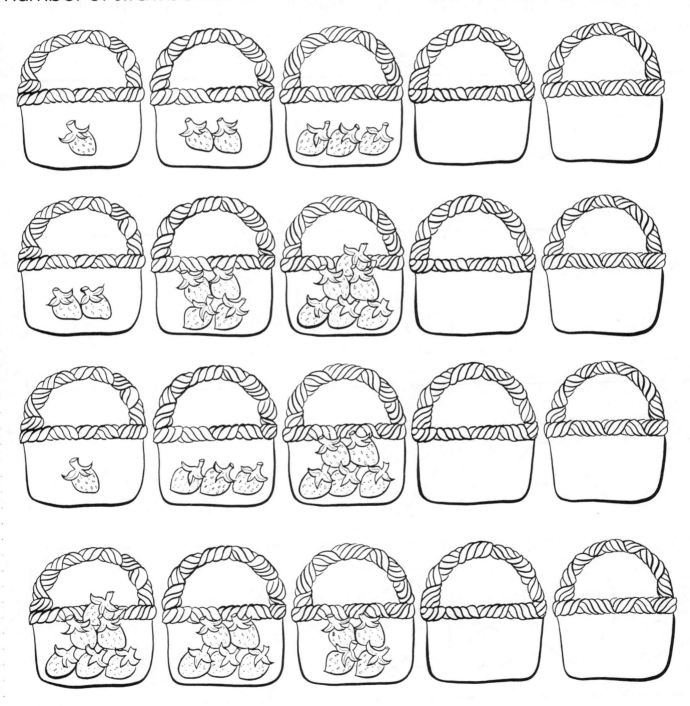

# Stringing It Along

Complete each pattern. Color the  **red** and the  **pink**.

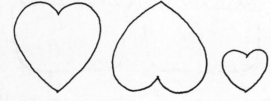

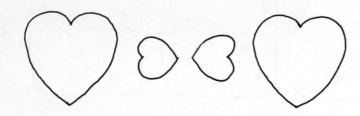

Stars change as they get older. They start out big and then shrink. As they shrink, they change color. Color the stars the correct color.

red    orange    yellow    blue

Look at all of these stars. Color each star the correct color. Then draw a circle around the youngest stars and a box around the oldest ones.

# Size Search

Circle each size word. Write the correct number by each picture.
Color each picture the correct color.

1. a long, brown snake

2. a little, red heart

3. a tall, green tree

4. a large, blue house

5. a small, orange gift

6. a short, yellow pencil

7. a big, purple tent

# Rainbow-Colored Numbers

Color: 1's—red
2's—blue
3's—yellow
4's—green
5's—orange

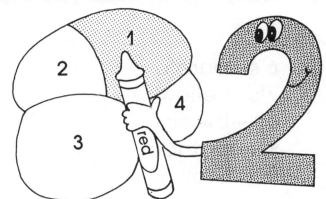

# One Beautiful Butterfly

Color: 6's—purple
7's—yellow
8's—black
9's—orange
10's—brown

# Clown Count

 the 🎈's:

| 1 - blue | 2 - orange | 3 - yellow | 4 - green |
| | 5 - purple | 6 - brown | |
| 7 - red | 8 - black | 9 - blue | 10 - purple |

Color clown, too!

# Number Express

Number the train.

Draw a line from the word to the number.

| seven | 1 |
| two | 8 |
| five | 3 |
| nine | 4 |
| six | 7 |
| four | 5 |
| one | 6 |
| three | 2 |
| eight | 9 |

Color train cars.　　one-**red**　　three-**green**　　five-**orange**

two-**blue**　　four-**yellow**　　six-**brown**

# Wintry Ride

Count each set of bears. Draw a line from each set to the sled that has the correct number.

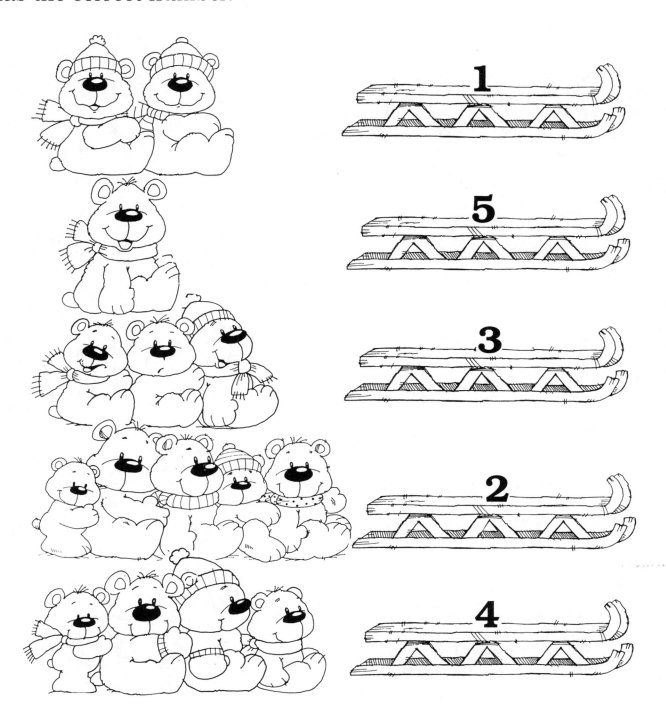

# Pack a Snack

Count each set of sandwiches. Draw a line from each set to the backpack that has the correct number.

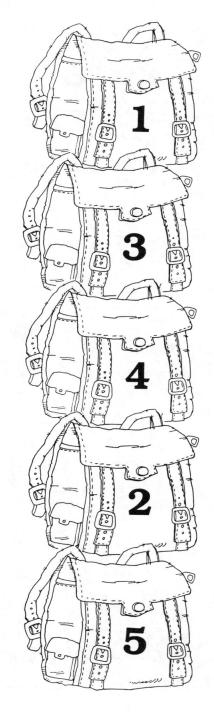

# Save Six

Color six animals.

Color six things that will grow.

Draw pictures of six of your favorite things.

# Sheepish Shepherd

Count the sheep on each hill. Then write that number on each tree.

# Beach Blanket Numbers

Count. Use the code to color the pictures.

1—blue     4—red     7—purple
2—yellow   5—orange   8—gray
3—green    6—brown    9—black

# School Scene

## How many?

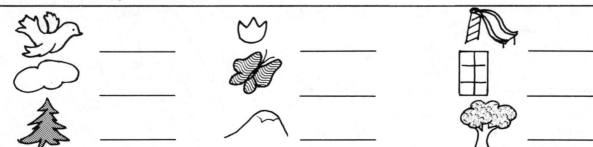

# Take an Animal Count!

Count the zoo animals in each box.  Match the number to the correct number word by drawing a line to it.  One is done for you.

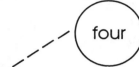

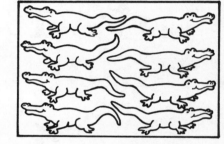

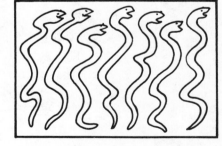

four

eight

one

ten

seven

two

six

three

nine

five

# Happy Hikers

Hike your way to camp. Trace a path through the maze by counting from **1** to **10** in the correct order. Color the picture.

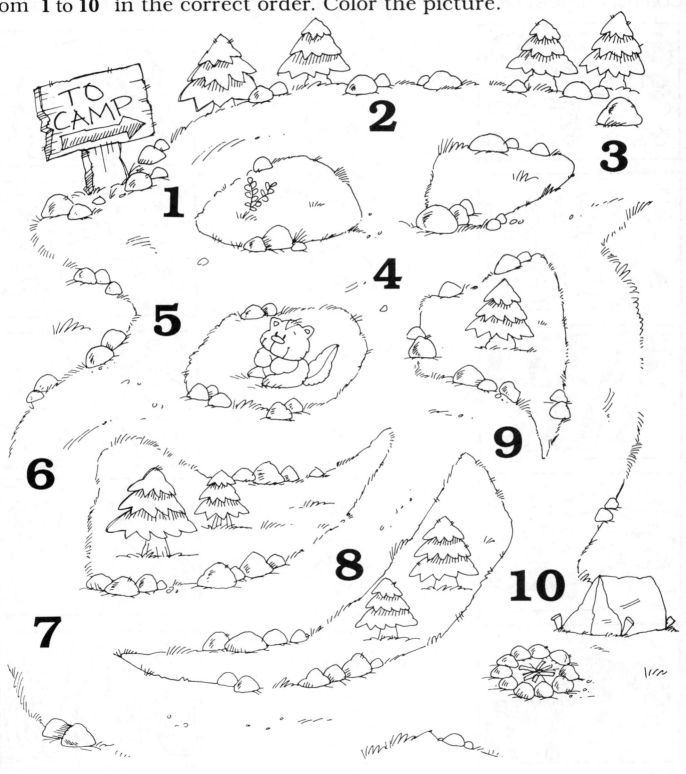

Join the dots in order.
Color the surprise.

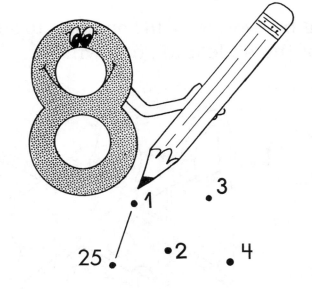

•1

•3

25•

•2      •4

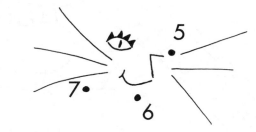

5
•

7•

•6

18•

•8

•19

17•

24•

16•

•23

20•

•9

•10

•21

15•      •22

•14      13•  )) •11
              12  ))

# Two for the Pool

Counting by twos, write the numbers to 50 in the waterdrops. Start at the top of the slide and go down.

# I'm Counting on You

Write and count by twos.

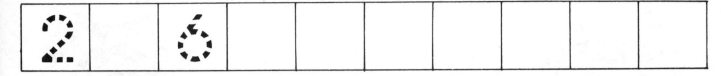

| 2 | 6 | | | | | | | |
|---|---|---|---|---|---|---|---|---|

Write and count by fives.

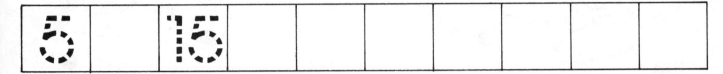

| 5 | 15 | | | | | | | |
|---|----|---|---|---|---|---|---|---|

Connect the dots by twos.

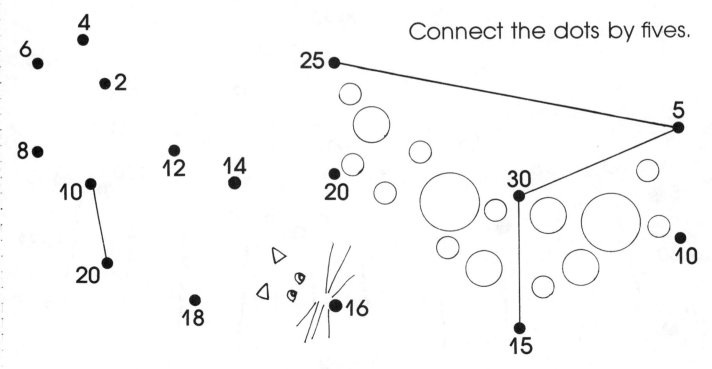

Connect the dots by fives.

# Count the Cookie Clues

Find out what holds something crumbly, but good! Counting by fives, connect the dots in order. Start with 5. Color the picture.

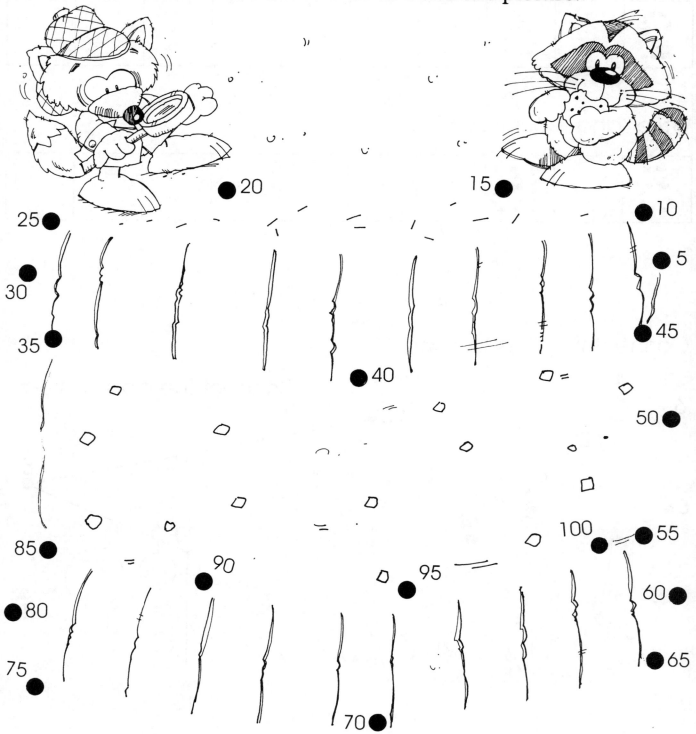

First Grade Bound © Carson-Dellosa • CD-704634

# Desert Trek

As you count by tens, color each canteen with the number you say to lead the camel to the watering hole.

# Caterpillar Count

Circle numbers counting by twos.

| 1, ②, 3, 4, 5, 6, 7, |
| 8, 9, 10, 11, 12, 13, |
| 14, 15, 16, 17, 18, 19, |
| 20, 21, 22, 23, 24 |

Count by twos.

2 , 4 , ___ , ___ , ___ , ___ , ___ , ___

Put △ around numbers counting by fives.

| 1, 2, 3, 4, △5△ 6, 7, 8, 9, |
| 10, 11, 12, 13, 14, 15, 16, |
| 17, 18, 19, 20, 21, 22, |
| 23, 24, 25, 26, 27, |
| 28, 29, 30, 31, 32, 33, |
| 34, 35, 36, 37, 38, 39, 40 |

Count by fives.

5 , 10 , ___ , ___ , ___ , ___ , ___ , ___

Put ☐ around numbers counting by tens.

| 1, 2, 3, 4, 5, 6, 7, 8, 9, [10,] 11, |
| 12, 13, 14, 15, 16, 17, 18, 19, |
| 20, 21, 22, 23, 24, 25, 26, |
| 27, 28, 29, 30, 31, 32, 33 |

Count by tens.

10 , ___ , ___ , ___ , ___ , ___ , ___ , ___

# Barking Up a Tree

Use counters.  Trace or draw each set you make.  Then, write how many in all.

How many?        How many more?        How many in all?

| 3 | + | 2 | = | ____ |

| 2 | + | 1 | = | ____ |

| 4 | + | 3 | = | ____ |

| 1 | + | 6 | = | ____ |

Think of a story for this picture.  Write how many in all.

| |
|---|
| ____ |
| in all |

## How Many in All?

2 + 2 = 4

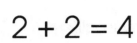

$$\begin{array}{r} 2 \\ + \ 2 \\ \hline 4 \end{array}$$

Write an addition sentence and a vertical fact for each picture story.
Find how many in all.

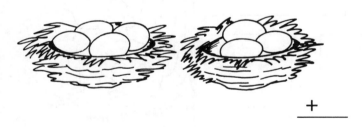

$$\begin{array}{r} \\ + \ \_\_ \\ \hline \phantom{0} \end{array}$$

___ + ___ = ___

$$\begin{array}{r} \\ + \ \_\_ \\ \hline \phantom{0} \end{array}$$

___ + ___ = ___

$$\begin{array}{r} \\ + \ \_\_ \\ \hline \phantom{0} \end{array}$$

___ + ___ = ___

$$\begin{array}{r} \\ + \ \_\_ \\ \hline \phantom{0} \end{array}$$

___ + ___ = ___

$$\begin{array}{r} \\ + \ \_\_ \\ \hline \phantom{0} \end{array}$$

___ + ___ = ___

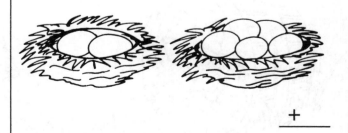

$$\begin{array}{r} \\ + \ \_\_ \\ \hline \phantom{0} \end{array}$$

___ + ___ = ___

# Addition Using Counters

**Example**    $2 + 1 = \underline{?}$

Use counters to add.

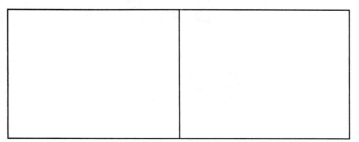

Put in 2.      Put in 1 more.

How many counters are there in all?   _3_

So, $2 + 1 = \underline{3}$ . The number that tells how many in all is called the **sum**. The sum of $2 + 1$ is 3.

Use counters to find each sum.

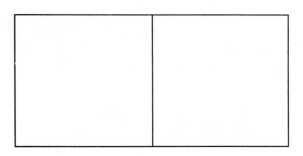

$2 + 4 = \underline{\phantom{000}}$

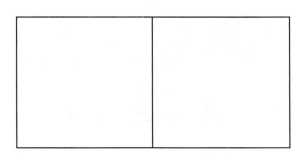

$5 + 2 = \underline{\phantom{000}}$

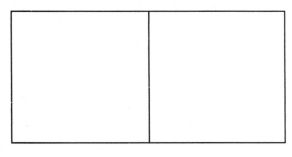

$3 + 3 = \underline{\phantom{000}}$

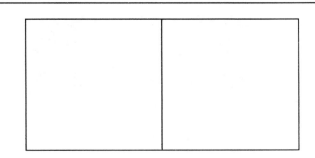

$3 + 4 = \underline{\phantom{000}}$

# Prehistoric Picture Problems

Circle the picture which matches the number sentence.

**1.**

$$1 + 2 = 3$$

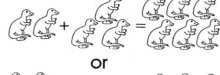

or

**2.**

$$2 + 3 = 5$$

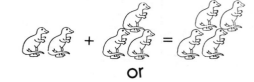

or

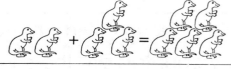

**3.**

$$4 + 2 = 6$$

or

**4.**

$$5 + 1 = 6$$

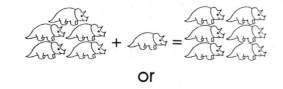

or

**5.**

$$3 + 4 = 7$$

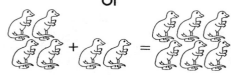

or

**6.**

$$6 + 1 = 7$$

or

First Grade Bound © Carson-Dellosa • CD-704634

# Alien Problems

Look at the pictures and finish the number sentences.

**1.**

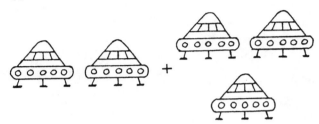

$2 + 3 = \underline{\phantom{5}}$

**2.**

$1 + 7 = \underline{\phantom{00}}$

**3.**

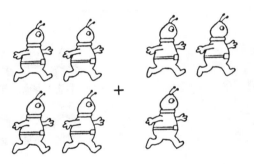

$4 + 3 = \underline{\phantom{00}}$

**4.**

$5 + 0 = \underline{\phantom{00}}$

**5.**

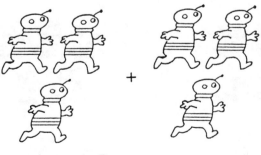

$3 + 3 = \underline{\phantom{00}}$

**6.**

$4 + 5 = \underline{\phantom{00}}$

# Bear Necessities

Draw in the missing pictures and finish the number sentences.

**1.**

$$1 + \underline{\phantom{2}} = 3$$

**2.**

$$3 + \underline{\phantom{2}} = 5$$

**3.**

$$5 + \underline{\phantom{2}} = 8$$

**4.**

$$3 + \underline{\phantom{2}} = 6$$

**5.**

$$2 + \underline{\phantom{2}} = 7$$

**6.**

$$4 + \underline{\phantom{2}} = 5$$

# The Missing Chickens

Draw in the missing pictures and finish the number sentences.

**1.**

_____1_____ + 2 = 3

**2.**

_____ + 3 = 6

**3.**

5 + _____ = 7

**4.**

_____ + 3 = 5

**5.**

_____ + 4 = 8

**6.**

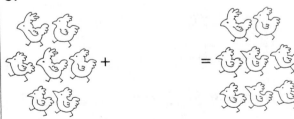

7 + _____ = 8

# How Many Robots in All?

Look at the pictures and finish the number sentences.

**1.**

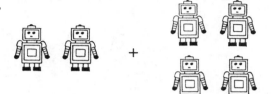

How many 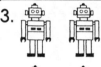's are there in all?

$2 + 4 = $ _____

**2.**

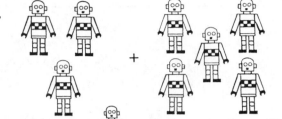

How many 's are there in all?

$3 + 5 = $ _____

**3.**

How many 's are there in all?

$4 + 3 = $ _____

**4.**

How many 's are there in all?

$4 + 1 = $ _____

**5.**

How many 's are there in all?

$2 + 5 = $ _____

**6.**

How many 's are there in all?

$4 + 4 = $ _____

# How Many Rabbits?

Look at the pictures and finish the number sentences.

1.

How many 's are there in all?

$1 + 1 = \underline{2}$

2.

How many 's are there in all?

$3 + 6 = \underline{\hspace{1.5cm}}$

3.

How many 's are there in all?

$6 + 1 = \underline{\hspace{1.5cm}}$

4.

How many 's are there in all?

$3 + 4 = \underline{\hspace{1.5cm}}$

5.

How many 's are there in all?

$4 + 5 = \underline{\hspace{1.5cm}}$

6.

How many 's are there in all?

$2 + 3 = \underline{\hspace{1.5cm}}$

# Bee Addition

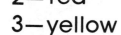 3 + 1 =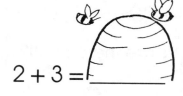

Add. Use code to color each bee.

| 2—red | 4—blue |
|---|---|
| 3—yellow | 5—green |

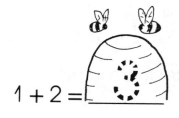

1 + 2 = _____

2 + 3 = _____

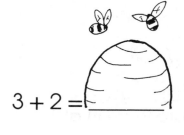

3 + 2 = _____

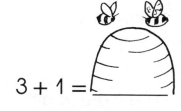

3 + 1 = _____

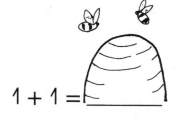

1 + 1 = _____

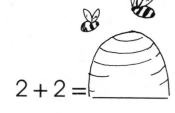

2 + 2 = _____

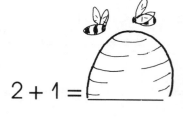

2 + 1 = _____

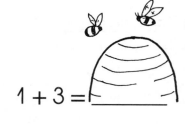

1 + 3 = _____

# Lumberjack Facts

Add.

If the answer equals **1**, color the space **red**.
If the answer equals **2**, color the space **yellow**.
If the answer equals **3**, color the space **black**.
If the answer equals **4**, color the space **blue**.
If the answer equals **5**, color the space **brown**.
If the answer equals **6**, color the space **green**.

# Creature Count

$$5 + 1 = 6$$

$4 + 6 =$

$1 + 9 =$

$7 + 1 =$

$7 + 3 =$

$5 + 2 =$

$6 + 1 =$

$8 + 2 =$

$3 + 5 =$

$6 + 3 =$

$6 + 2 =$

$4 + 5 =$

$1 + 7 =$

# Beary Good

Put counters on each bear to show the addition. Write the sums.

3 + 2 = ___        5 + 0 = ___        1 + 6 = ___        4 + 2 = ___

$$\begin{array}{r} 6 \\ +\ 1 \\ \hline \end{array} \qquad \begin{array}{r} 3 \\ +\ 4 \\ \hline \end{array} \qquad \begin{array}{r} 2 \\ +\ 3 \\ \hline \end{array} \qquad \begin{array}{r} 5 \\ +\ 2 \\ \hline \end{array} \qquad \begin{array}{r} 7 \\ +\ 1 \\ \hline \end{array} \qquad \begin{array}{r} 0 \\ +\ 2 \\ \hline \end{array}$$

$$\begin{array}{r} 8 \\ +\ 0 \\ \hline \end{array} \qquad \begin{array}{r} 4 \\ +\ 5 \\ \hline \end{array} \qquad \begin{array}{r} 3 \\ +\ 6 \\ \hline \end{array} \qquad \begin{array}{r} 2 \\ +\ 6 \\ \hline \end{array} \qquad \begin{array}{r} 3 \\ +\ 5 \\ \hline \end{array} \qquad \begin{array}{r} 6 \\ +\ 2 \\ \hline \end{array}$$

# Animal Addition

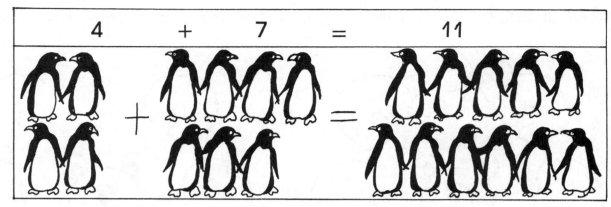

4 + 7 = 11

Add.

3 + 9 = __12__

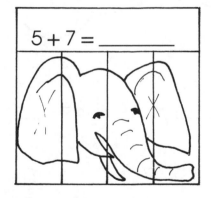

6 + 7 = _____

6 + 5 = _____

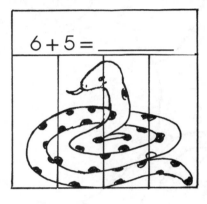

5 + 7 = _____

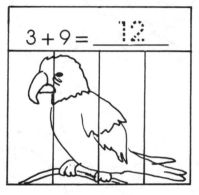

4 + 9 = _____

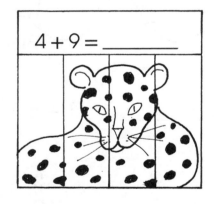

9 + 6 = _____

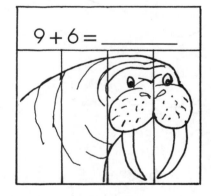

7 + 7 = _____

7 + 8 = _____

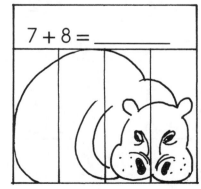

6 + 8 = _____

# Add the Apples

Match.

| | |
|---|---|
| 8 + 2 | 15 |
| 9 + 6 | 4 |
| 2 + 2 | 10 |

| | |
|---|---|
| 1 + 2 | 11 |
| 6 + 7 | 3 |
| 5 + 6 | 13 |

| | |
|---|---|
| 6 + 2 | 8 |
| 1 + 1 | 6 |
| 1 + 5 | 2 |

| | |
|---|---|
| 3 + 2 | 10 |
| 6 + 8 | 14 |
| 5 + 5 | 5 |

| | |
|---|---|
| 6 + 6 | 12 |
| 6 + 3 | 9 |
| 3 + 4 | 7 |

| | |
|---|---|
| 7 + 2 | 15 |
| 6 + 9 | 9 |
| 12 + 1 | 13 |

| | |
|---|---|
| 10 + 1 | 14 |
| 9 + 5 | 8 |
| 7 + 1 | 11 |

# What's the Difference?

| Example | $5 - 2 = \underline{?}$ |

Use counters to subtract.

Put in 5.  Take away 2.

How many counters are left? _3_

So, $5 - 2 = 3$.  The number that tells how many are left is called the **difference**.  The difference of $5 - 2$ is 3.

Use counters to find each difference.

$6 - 3 = \underline{\phantom{0}}$

$5 - 1 = \underline{\phantom{0}}$

$5 - 3 = \underline{\phantom{0}}$

$4 - 2 = \underline{\phantom{0}}$

# Counting Kittens

Use counters. Make a set, then take away. Write how many are left.

_____
are left.

Put in 4. Take away 1.

_____
are left.

Put in 5. Take away 2.

_____
are left.

Put in 6. Take away 1.

_____
are left.

Put in 7. Take away 3.

Think of a story
for this picture.
Write how
many are left.

_____
are left.

# Transportation Problems

Circle the picture which matches the number sentence. Then finish the number sentence.

**1.**

or

$$4 - 1 = \underline{\quad}$$

**2.**

or

$$6 - 2 = \underline{\quad}$$

**3.**

or

$$5 - 3 = \underline{\quad}$$

**4.**

or

$$7 - 3 = \underline{\quad}$$

**5.**

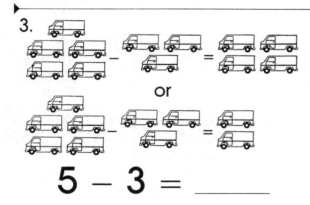

or

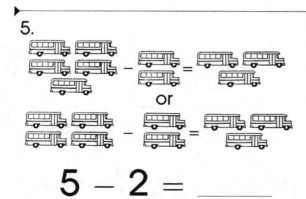

$$5 - 2 = \underline{\quad}$$

**6.**

or

$$7 - 5 = \underline{\quad}$$

# Sea Creature Subtraction

Look at the pictures and finish the number sentences.

1.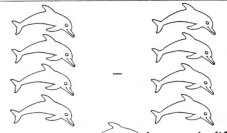

How many 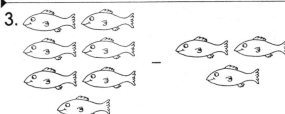's are left?

$$4 - 4 = \underline{0}$$

2.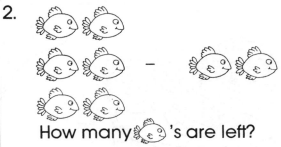

How many 🐟's are left?

$$6 - 2 = \underline{\hspace{1cm}}$$

3.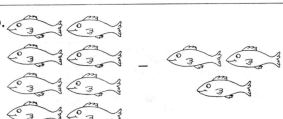

How many 🐟's are left?

$$7 - 3 = \underline{\hspace{1cm}}$$

4.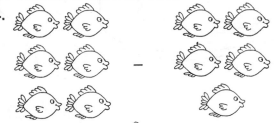

How many 🐟's are left?

$$6 - 5 = \underline{\hspace{1cm}}$$

5.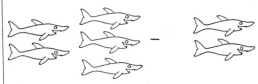

How many 🐟's are left?

$$8 - 3 = \underline{\hspace{1cm}}$$

6.

How many 🦈's are left?

$$5 - 2 = \underline{\hspace{1cm}}$$

# Nutty Subtraction

Count the nuts.
Write answer on blank.
Circle problems with same answer.

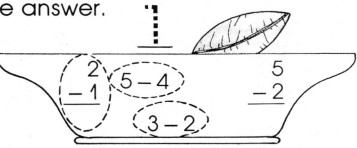

$1$

$$\begin{array}{r} 2 \\ -1 \end{array}$$   $5 - 4$

$3 - 2$

$$\begin{array}{r} 5 \\ -2 \end{array}$$

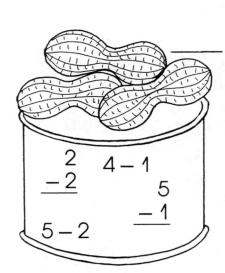

$$\begin{array}{r} 2 \\ -2 \end{array}$$   $4 - 1$

$$\begin{array}{r} 5 \\ -1 \end{array}$$

$5 - 2$

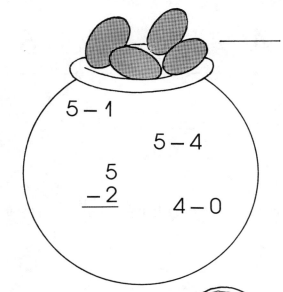

$5 - 1$

$5 - 4$

$$\begin{array}{r} 5 \\ -2 \end{array}$$

$4 - 0$

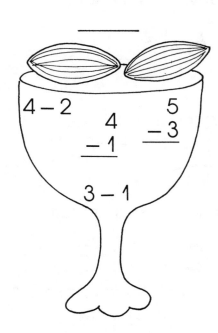

$4 - 2$   $$\begin{array}{r} 4 \\ -1 \end{array}$$   $$\begin{array}{r} 5 \\ -3 \end{array}$$

$3 - 1$

$5 - 0$   $$\begin{array}{r} 2 \\ -2 \end{array}$$

$$\begin{array}{r} 5 \\ -1 \end{array}$$   $$\begin{array}{r} 4 \\ -3 \end{array}$$

First Grade Bound © Carson-Dellosa • CD-704634

# Robins and Worms

$$3 - 2 = 1$$

$$\begin{array}{r} 3 \\ -2 \\ \hline 1 \end{array}$$

5 – 1 = _____     3 – 1 = _____     5 – 2 = _____

4 – 1 = _____     2 – 1 = _____     4 – 2 = _____

3 – 2 = _____     4 – 3 = _____     5 – 3 = _____

## Subtract. Use code to color worms.

**1—red**     **3—yellow**
**2—orange**     **4—brown**

$$5 - 1 = \bigcirc$$
$$\begin{array}{r} 5 \\ -1 \\ \hline \end{array}$$

$$4 - 2 = \bigcirc$$
$$\begin{array}{r} 4 \\ -2 \\ \hline \end{array}$$
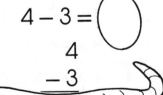

$$5 - 2 = \bigcirc$$
$$\begin{array}{r} 5 \\ -2 \\ \hline \end{array}$$
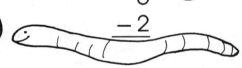

$$3 - 1 = \bigcirc$$
$$\begin{array}{r} 3 \\ -1 \\ \hline \end{array}$$
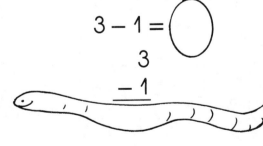

$$4 - 3 = \bigcirc$$
$$\begin{array}{r} 4 \\ -3 \\ \hline \end{array}$$

$$5 - 3 = \bigcirc$$
$$\begin{array}{r} 5 \\ -3 \\ \hline \end{array}$$
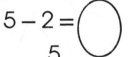

$$2 - 1 = \bigcirc$$
$$\begin{array}{r} 2 \\ -1 \\ \hline \end{array}$$
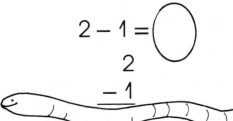

$$4 - 1 = \bigcirc$$
$$\begin{array}{r} 4 \\ -1 \\ \hline \end{array}$$

$$3 - 2 = \bigcirc$$
$$\begin{array}{r} 3 \\ -2 \\ \hline \end{array}$$
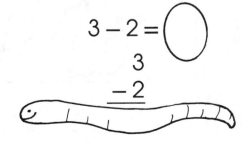
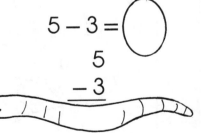

# "Berry" Tasty

Subtract.

If the answer is **0**, color the space **green**.

If the answer is **1**, color the space **brown**.

If the answer is **2**, color the space **blue**.

If the answer is **3**, color the space **purple**.

If the answer is **4**, color the space **black**.

If the answer is **5**, color the space **pink**.

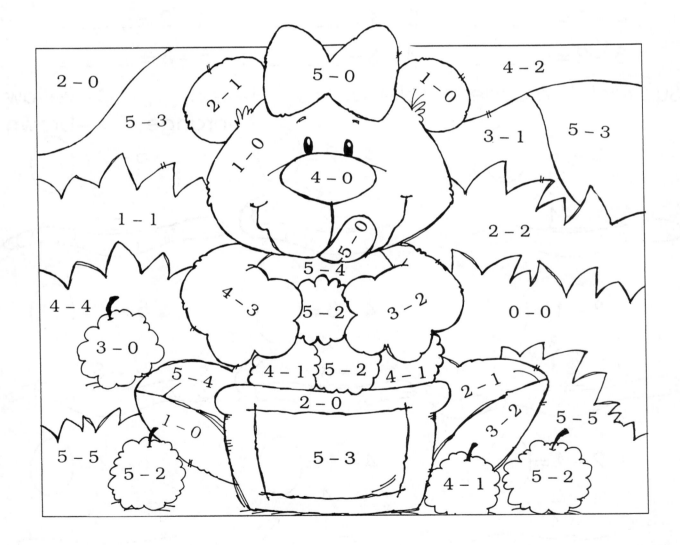

# Bubbly Baths

Subtract. Write each answer on the rubber duck.

5 – 4

1 – 0

4 – 2

2 – 1

3 – 1

3 – 2

4 – 1

1 – 1

5 – 1

5 – 2

# Fewer Fruits

$9 - 2 = 7$

$$\begin{array}{r} 7 \\ -\ 1 \\ \hline 6 \end{array}$$

Subtract. Use code to color.

6—orange  9—green
7—red  10—purple
8—yellow

$11 - 1 =$

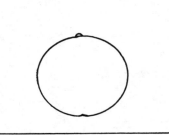

$$\begin{array}{r} 9 \\ -\ 1 \\ \hline \end{array}$$

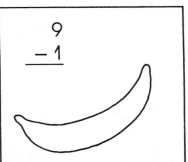

$8 - 1 =$

$10 - 4 =$

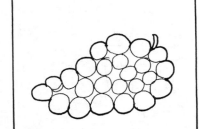

$$\begin{array}{r} 9 \\ -\ 2 \\ \hline \end{array}$$

$$\begin{array}{r} 10 \\ -\ 1 \\ \hline \end{array}$$

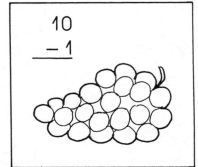

$10 - 2 =$

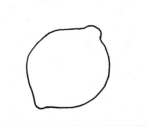

$11 - 2 =$

$$\begin{array}{r} 10 \\ -\ 3 \\ \hline \end{array}$$

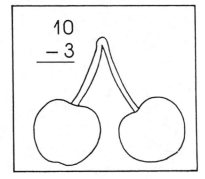

First Grade Bound © Carson-Dellosa • CD-704634

# Sweet Treats

Count the candy.
Write number on blank.
Circle problems with same answer.

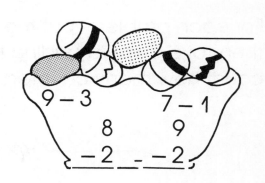

_____

$9 - 3$        $7 - 1$
  8           9
$-2$      $-\ -2$

_____

$10 - 1$

    $10 - 4$
  11
$-2$      9
        $-1$

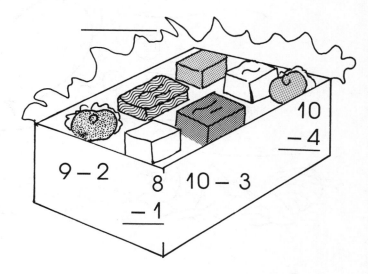

_____

                    10
                   $-4$
$9 - 2$    8    $10 - 3$
        $-1$

_____

10    $7 - 2$    8
$-4$           $-2$

     $8 - 2$

_____

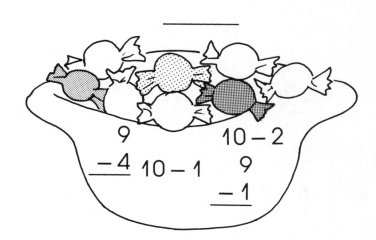

_____

  9        $10 - 2$
$-4$  $10 - 1$  9
              $-1$

# A Whale of a Job!

For each problem, put the number of counters needed in the water, then take away by sliding the numbers into the whale's mouth. Then, count how many counters are left in the water to find the difference.

| 7 | 9 | 6 | 5 | 8 |
|---|---|---|---|---|
| − 3 | − 2 | − 4 | − 2 | − 3 |

| 9 | 6 | 7 | 8 | 5 |
|---|---|---|---|---|
| − 3 | − 3 | − 5 | − 2 | − 1 |

8 − 4 = _____          6 − 2 = _____          7 − 4 = _____

First Grade Bound © Carson-Dellosa • CD-704634

# Hop Along Numbers

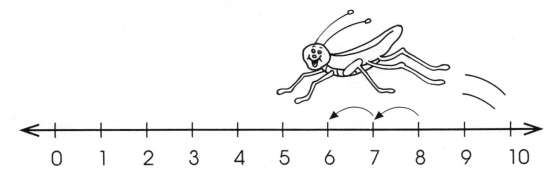

Use the number line to **count back**.

8, __7__ , __6__        6, ____ , ____

5, ____ , ____        7, ____ , ____ , ____

Use the number line to count back to find each difference.

Example: $9 - 2 = \underline{?}$    Start with 9. Count back 2.

9, ____ , ____        $9 - 2 = $ ____

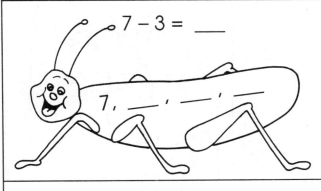

$7 - 3 = $ ___

7, ____ , ____

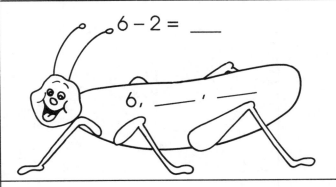

$6 - 2 = $ ___

6, ____ , ____

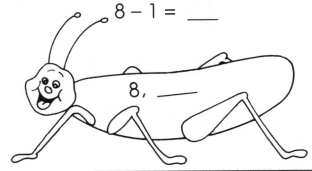

$8 - 1 = $ ___

8, ____

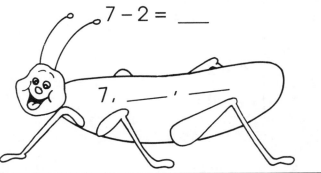

$7 - 2 = $ ___

7, ____ , ____

# Crayon Count

Count the crayons. Write the number on the blank.
Circle problems that equal that number.

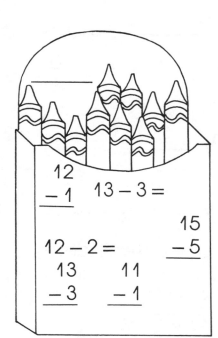

_____

12
− 1

13 − 3 =

12 − 2 =

15
− 5

13      11
− 3    − 1

9

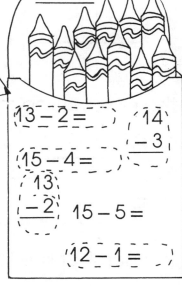

11

13 − 2 =

15 − 4 =

13
− 2

14
− 3

15 − 5 =

12 − 1 =

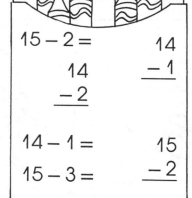

_____

15 − 2 =

14
− 2

14 − 1 =

15 − 3 =

14
− 1

15
− 2

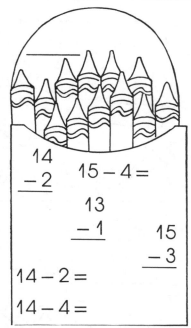

_____

14
− 2

15 − 4 =

13
− 1

15
− 3

14 − 2 =

14 − 4 =

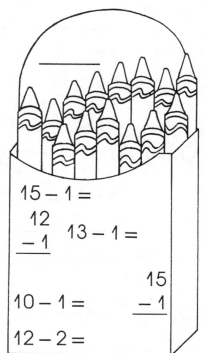

_____

15 − 1 =

12
− 1

13 − 1 =

10 − 1 =

12 − 2 =

15
− 1

First Grade Bound © Carson-Dellosa • CD-704634

# Turtle Math

Color:
2—red
3—blue
4—yellow
5—green

# It's Show Time

It's time for Packy and Dermit to perform. Look at the problems.

Write **+** or **−** on each peanut to make the problem correct. Then trace a path from peanut to peanut, connecting each elephant to the correct stool. For Packy, connect all of the **+** problems. For Dermit, connect all of the **−** problems.

Packy

Dermit

$3 \bigcirc 2 = 5$

$10 \bigcirc 8 = 2$

$2 \bigcirc 6 = 8$

$8 \bigcirc 2 = 6$

$7 \bigcirc 3 = 4$

$5 \bigcirc 4 = 9$

$9 \bigcirc 4 = 5$

$5 \bigcirc 5 = 10$

$10 \bigcirc 3 = 7$

$3 \bigcirc 3 = 0$

$7 \bigcirc 5 = 2$

$9 \bigcirc 1 = 10$

$6 \bigcirc 4 = 10$

$6 \bigcirc 3 = 3$

$5 \bigcirc 2 = 7$

$5 \bigcirc 3 = 8$

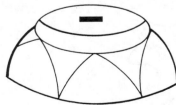

−

+

$2 \bigcirc 7 = 9$

# Puppy Problems

Look at the pictures and finish the number sentences.

1. $5 \oplus 6 = \underline{11}$

2. $11 \bigcirc 4 = \underline{\hphantom{00}}$

3. $12 \bigcirc 7 = \underline{\hphantom{00}}$

4. $7 \bigcirc 6 = \underline{\hphantom{00}}$

5. $5 \bigcirc 5 = \underline{\hphantom{00}}$

6. $8 \bigcirc 6 = \underline{\hphantom{00}}$

Name _____

# Calling All Cats

**Addition and Subtraction**

Look at the pictures and finish the number sentences.

1.

How many 's are there in all?

$7 \oplus 4 = \underline{11}$

2.

How many 's are there in all?

$6 \bigcirc 8 = \underline{\hphantom{000}}$

3.

How many 's are there in all?

$11 \bigcirc 2 = \underline{\hphantom{000}}$

4.

How many 's are left?

$13 \bigcirc 7 = \underline{\hphantom{000}}$

5.

How many 's are left?

$9 \bigcirc 6 = \underline{\hphantom{000}}$

6.

How many 's are left?

$12 \bigcirc 8 = \underline{\hphantom{000}}$

First Grade Bound © Carson-Dellosa • CD-704634

# What Was the Question?

Draw a line under the question that matches the picture. Then finish the number sentence.

1.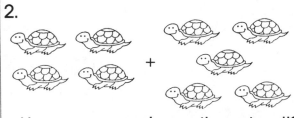

How many 🐸's are there in all?

How many 🐸's are left?

$11 - 7 = \underline{4}$

2.

How many 🐢's are there in all?

How many 🐢's are left?

$4 + 5 = \underline{\hspace{1cm}}$

3.

How many 🍄's are there in all?

How many 🍄's are left?

$8 - 3 = \underline{\hspace{1cm}}$

4.

How many 🍄's are there in all?

How many 🍄's are left?

$10 - 4 = \underline{\hspace{1cm}}$

5.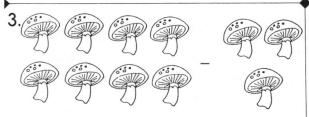

How many 🐌's are there in all?

How many 🐌's are left?

$5 + 6 = \underline{\hspace{1cm}}$

6.

How many 🐸's are there in all?

How many 🐸's are left?

$8 + 4 = \underline{\hspace{1cm}}$

# Sunny Day Delight

Draw a line under the question that matches the picture.
Then finish the number sentence.

1.

How many 🍦's are there in all?
How many 🍦's are left?

$6 + 6 =$ ___12___

2.

How many 🍦's are there in all?
How many 🍦's are left?

$13 - 4 =$ _____

3.

How many 🍦's are there in all?
How many 🍦's are left?

$9 + 5 =$ _____

4.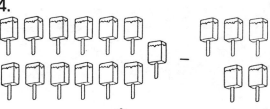

How many 🍡's are there in all?
How many 🍡's are left?

$13 - 5 =$ _____

5.

How many 🍦's are there in all?
How many 🍦's are left?

$7 + 7 =$ _____

6.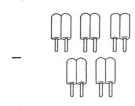

How many 🍧's are there in all?
How many 🍧's are left?

$9 - 5 =$ _____

# Fishing for Answers

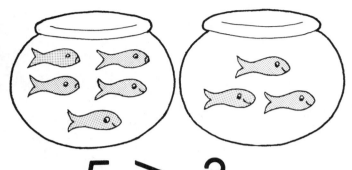

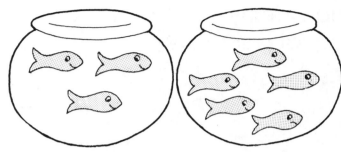

## 5 > 3
5 is **greater than** 3.

## 3 < 5
3 is **less than** 5.

Fill in number line.

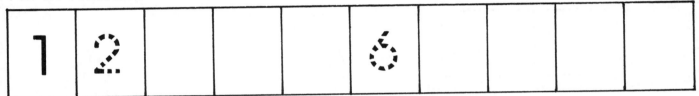

| 1 | 2 | | | | 6 | | | | |

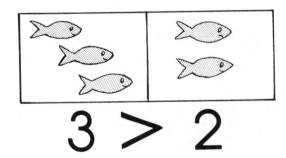

## 3 > 2

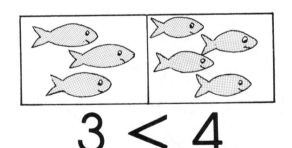

## 3 < 4

Write > or <. Use number line to help you.

| 5 ____ 2 | 1 ____ 7 | 1 ____ 9 | 8 ____ 5 |
| 3 ____ 4 | 9 ____ 3 | 8 ____ 7 | 2 ____ 4 |
| 6 ____ 5 | 5 ____ 3 | 5 ____ 7 | 3 ____ 5 |
| 7 ____ 3 | 7 ____ 6 | 2 ____ 8 | 4 ____ 2 |

Name _____

How many equal parts?  2

 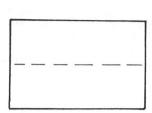 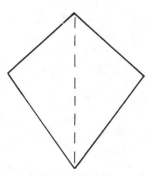

Color shapes with 2 equal parts.

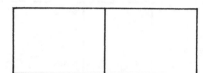 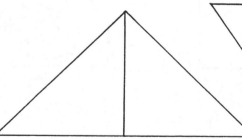

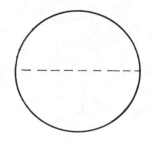  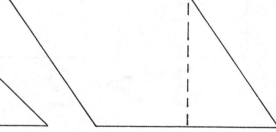

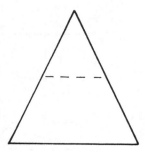 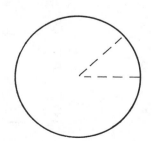 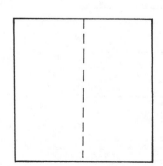

Name _____

How many equal parts? __3__

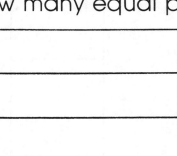

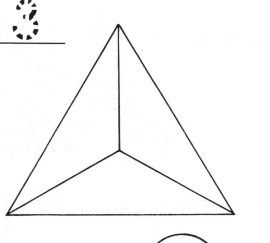

Color shapes with 3 equal parts.

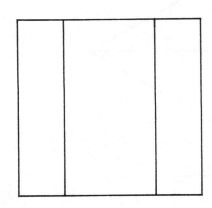

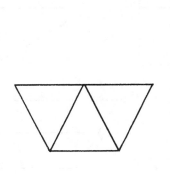

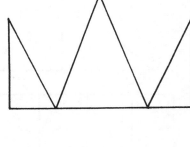

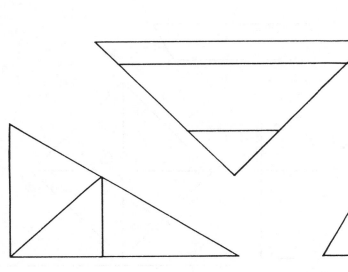

How many equal parts? ____4____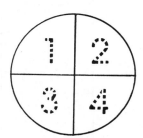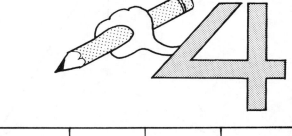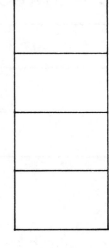

## Color shapes with 4 equal parts.

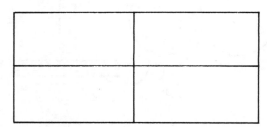 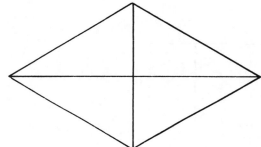

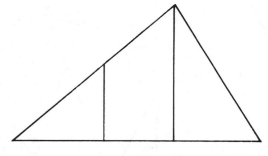 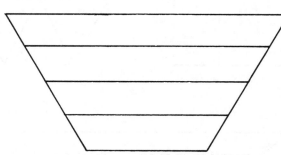

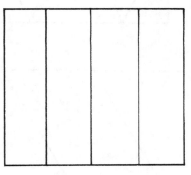  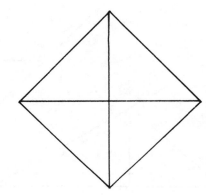

# A Race!

first

second

third

fourth

fifth

sixth

seventh

Write the correct word to tell where each runner placed in the race.

1.  _____

2. _____

3. _____

4.  _____

5. _____

6. _____

7.  _____

**Flip Fun!**  Draw a prize you would like to receive for winning a race.

# Flags First

Color the **ninth** flag red.
Write **O** on the **second** flag.
Color the **eighth** flag blue.
Write **D** on the **fourth** flag.
Color the **sixth** flag yellow.
Write **G** on the **first** flag.
Color the **tenth** flag purple.
Write **O** on the **third** flag.
Color the **seventh** flag green.
Color the **fifth** flag orange.

# Balls of All Kinds

Color second
ball **brown**.

Color sixth
ball **yellow**.

 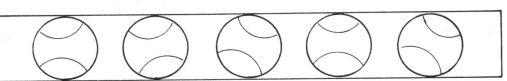

Color fourth
ball **orange**.

Color first
ball **black**.

Color third
ball **blue**.

Color fifth
ball **green**.

Color seventh
ball **purple**.

Color eighth
ball **pink**.

# An African Ant

1. Read each sentence and write the letter on the ant.

2. Then write each letter in order to find the answer to the riddle at the bottom.

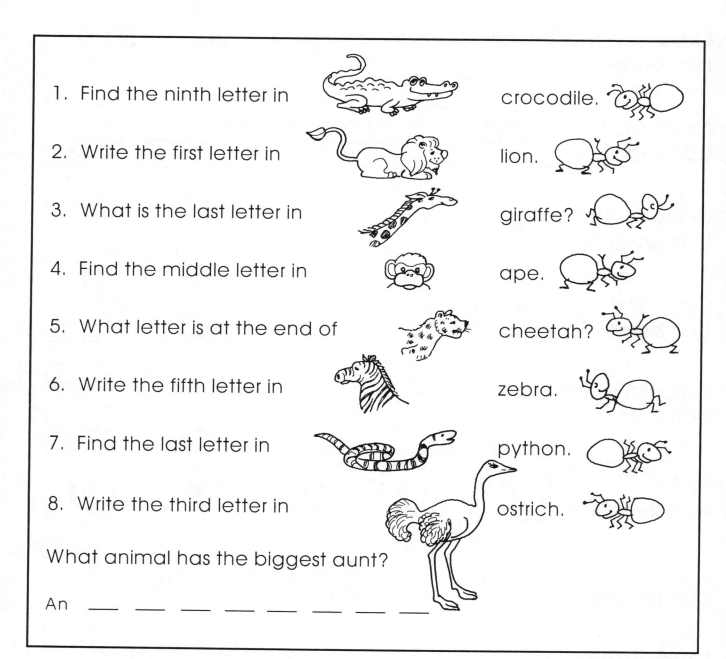

1. Find the ninth letter in          crocodile.

2. Write the first letter in          lion.

3. What is the last letter in          giraffe?

4. Find the middle letter in          ape.

5. What letter is at the end of          cheetah?

6. Write the fifth letter in          zebra.

7. Find the last letter in          python.

8. Write the third letter in          ostrich.

What animal has the biggest aunt?

An __ __ __ __ __ __ __ __

First Grade Bound © Carson-Dellosa • CD-704634

# Henny Penny

1¢   1 penny
     1 cent

## How much money?

Example

1¢ 1¢ 1¢
1¢ 1¢ = 5 ¢

1¢ 1¢ 1¢ 1¢
1¢ 1¢ = ☐ ¢

1¢ 1¢ = ☐ ¢

1¢ 1¢ 1¢ = ☐ ¢

1¢ 1¢ 1¢
1¢ = ☐ ¢

1¢ 1¢ 1¢ 1¢
1¢ 1¢ 1¢ 1¢ = ☐ ¢

1¢ 1¢ 1¢ 1¢ 1¢ 1¢ 1¢ = ☐ ¢

# Nickel Pickles

**5¢** 5 cents
1 nickel

How much money?

**5¢** **5¢**

**5¢** = **15** ¢

Count __5__ , __10__ , __15__

**5¢** **5¢** = ☐ ¢

Count____ , ____

**5¢** **5¢** **5¢**

**5¢** **5¢** = ☐ ¢

Count____ , ____ , ____

____ , ____

**5¢** **5¢** **5¢** **5¢**

**5¢** **5¢** **5¢** = ☐ ¢

Count____ , ____ , ____

____ , ____ , ____

**5¢** **5¢**

**5¢** **5¢** = ☐ ¢

Count____ , ____ , ____

____ , ____

**5¢** **5¢** **5¢**

**5¢** **5¢** **5¢** = ☐ ¢

Count____ , ____ , ____

____ , ____ , ____

# Cent-erpillars

Count the coins on each "cent"erpillar.

_17_ ¢

_____ ¢

_____ ¢

_____ ¢

_____ ¢

_____ ¢

_____ ¢

_____ ¢

_____ ¢

_____ ¢

# Marching Dimes

Come march with my dime friends and me!

Count by tens.

___10___ ¢   _____ ¢   _____ ¢

_____   _____   _____   _____

Count by tens. Write the number. Make a circle around the group which is **more**.

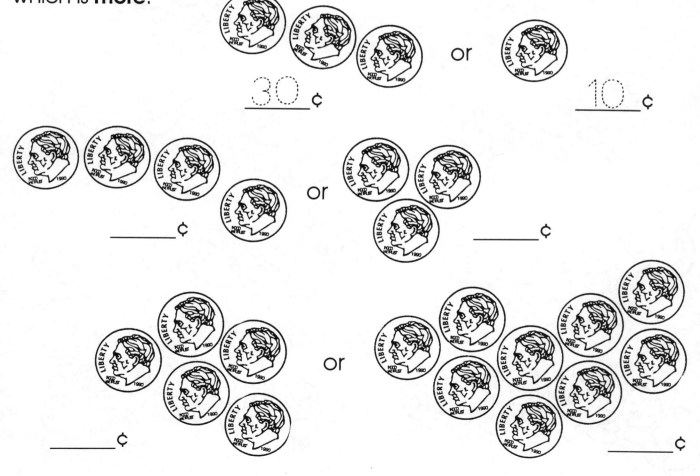

___30___ ¢                 or                 ___10___ ¢

_____ ¢                 or                 _____ ¢

_____ ¢                 or                 _____ ¢

First Grade Bound © Carson-Dellosa • CD-704634

Name _____

## Circle the coins to equal the right amount.

Example

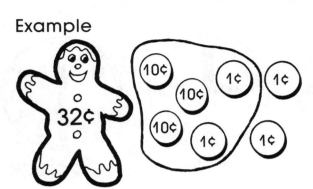

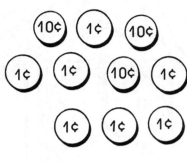

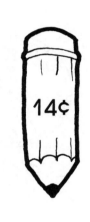

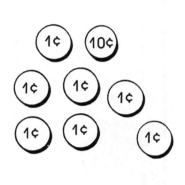

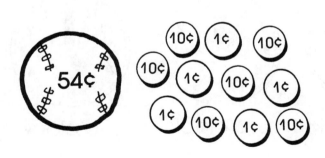

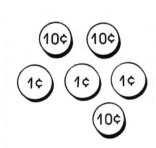

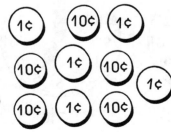

# Hickory Dickory Dock

## What time is it?

___o'clock     ___o'clock     ___o'clock

___o'clock     ___o'clock     ___o'clock

___o'clock     ___o'clock     ___o'clock

___o'clock     ___o'clock     ___o'clock

# Timely News

Cut out the newspapers at the bottom of the page. Paste each newspaper below the correct clock.

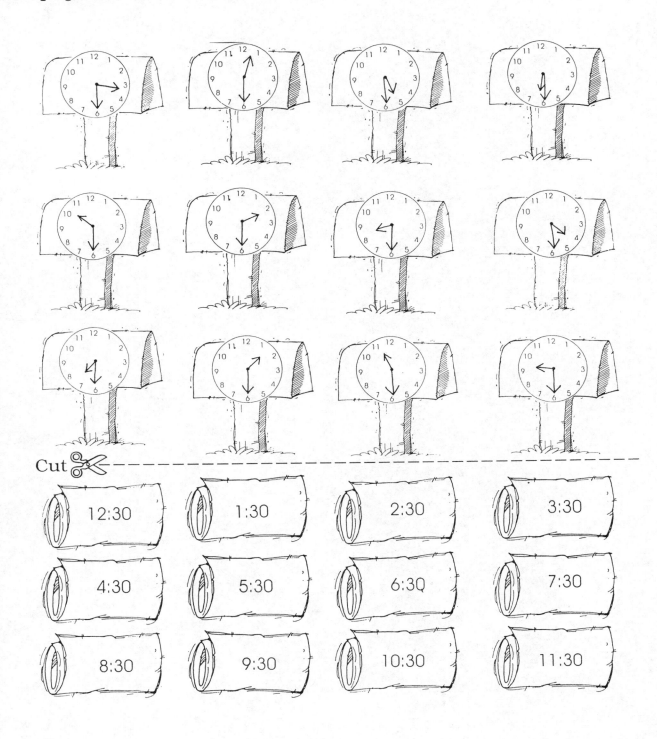

Cut ✂

| 12:30 | 1:30 | 2:30 | 3:30 |
| 4:30 | 5:30 | 6:30 | 7:30 |
| 8:30 | 9:30 | 10:30 | 11:30 |

# Sock Clocks

Draw the hands on the sock clocks.

1:30

7:00

4:30

10:00

3:30

9:30

4:00

2:30

6:00

# It's About Time

There are many ways we measure time. A year is made of 365 days. A week has seven days. A day has 24 hours. An hour is made of 60 minutes. A minute is made of 60 seconds. A second goes very quickly. Can you blink your eyes in one second?

| day | year | minute | week | hour |

**Write.**

1 ↓ 365 days make a **y** __ __ __.

2 → Seven days make a **w** __ __ __.

3 → 24 hours make a **d** __ __.

4 → 60 minutes make an **h** __ __ __.

5 ↓ 60 seconds make a **m** __ __ __ __ __.

Write the answers in the puzzle above.

**Check.**

The words in the puzzle tell about ☐ money.
☐ time.

• Write a list of what you can do in **two** minutes.

# Fun Days

There are seven days in a week. Saturday and Sunday are the weekend days. You go to school the other five days. Which day do you like best?

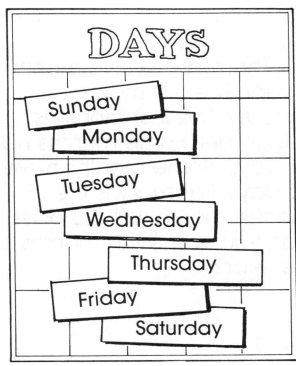

DAYS

Sunday
Monday
Tuesday
Wednesday
Thursday
Friday
Saturday

How many days are in a week?

six        seven        ten

Which two days make a weekend?

| Saturday |
| Thursday |
| Sunday |

_____

– – – – – – – – – – – – – – –

_____

– – – – – – – – – – – – – – –

_____

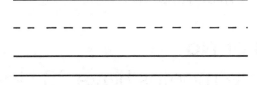 the five days you go to school.

• Draw and color what you do on a weekend.

# Hmm, What Month Is It?

There are twelve months in a year. The first month is January. The last month is December. Some months have 31 days. Some months have 30 days. February is the shortest month with 28 days. Can you name the months of the year?

☐ April
☐ October
☐ December
☐ July
☐ March
1 January
☐ May
☐ September
☐ June
☐ February
☐ August
☐ November

**Check.**

How many months are in a year?

☐ five
☐ nine
☐ twelve

**Write.**

_____          _____
first month                  last month

**Circle.**

Yes or No

| | | |
|---|---|---|
| Some months have 30 days. | Yes | No |
| Some months have 31 days. | Yes | No |
| February is the longest month. | Yes | No |
| February has 28 days. | Yes | No |

Write **1-12** in the ☐'s to put the months in order.

• Write the names of the twelve months in the correct order.

# Leaf Study

Put a leaf under the box on this paper. Rub the paper with the side of your crayon. Measure your leaf.

This is a rubbing of my leaf.

1. The color of my leaf is _____ .

2. My leaf is _____ cm wide and _____ cm long.

3. My leaf feels like _____ .

4. I found my leaf _____ .

# Math Checklist

Read the following skills aloud. Ask your child to place a check mark in each box once he or she has mastered the first grade skill.

- ☐ I know shapes such as circles, squares, rectangles, triangles, rhombuses, ovals, and hearts.

    I understand size words such as big, medium, and small.
- ☐ I can identify and create patterns.
- ☐ I can identify numbers and read number words.
- ☐ I can count from **1** to **25**.
- ☐ I can count by twos, fives, and tens.
- ☐ I can add and subtract.
- ☐ I understand halves, thirds, and fourths.
- ☐ I can count by ordinal numbers, such as first, second, third, fourth, fifth, sixth, seventh, and eighth.
- ☐ I can identify and add money.
- ☐ I can identify length and use the correct measurement tools.
- ☐ I can tell time by the hour and half hour.
- ☐ I can identify days of the week and months of the year.

### Now, try these fun learning activities!
Try these hands-on activities for enhancing your child's learning and development. Be sure to encourage speaking, listening, touching, and active movement.

- Place several addition flash cards in a grid pattern on the floor. Have your child toss a beanbag onto a problem. Ask your child to say the correct answer to the problem aloud before tossing the beanbag again.
- Give your child a black and white drawing of a rainbow. Give oral clues using ordinal numbers telling your child how to color the rainbow.
- When your child plays with modeling dough, ask him or her to run a pretend pizza shop. Phone in orders for pizzas and specify whether they should be cut into halves or fourths. The shop might offer rectangular and circular pizzas.

First Grade Bound © Carson-Dellosa • CD-704634

# Answer Key

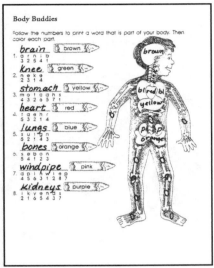

**Body Buddies**

Follow the numbers to print a word that is part of your body. Then color each part.

1. brain — brown
2. knee — green
3. stomach — yellow
4. heart — red
5. lungs — blue
6. bones — orange
7. windpipe — pink
8. kidneys — purple

**Page 10**

**Traffic Signs and Signals**

1. Color the STOP sign red.
2. Color the YIELD sign yellow.
3. DO NOT color the DO NOT ENTER sign.
4. Make the TRAFFIC LIGHT green.
5. Color the arrow on the ONE WAY sign black.
6. Color the WALK sign blue.

**Page 11**

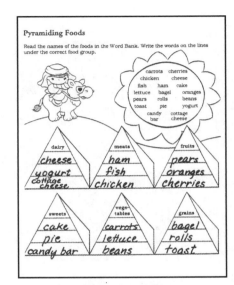

**Pyramiding Foods**

Read the names of the foods in the Word Bank. Write the words on the lines under the correct food group.

Word Bank: carrots, cherries, chicken, cheese, fish, ham, cake, lettuce, bagel, oranges, pears, rolls, beans, toast, pie, yogurt, candy bar, cottage cheese

dairy: cheese, yogurt, cottage cheese
meats: ham, fish, chicken
fruits: pears, oranges, cherries
sweets: cake, pie, candy bar
vegetables: carrots, lettuce, beans
grains: bagel, rolls, toast

**Page 12**

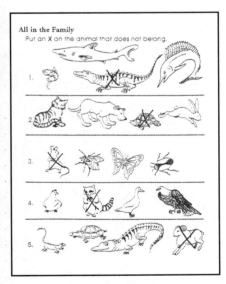

**All in the Family**

Put an X on the animal that does not belong.

**Page 13**

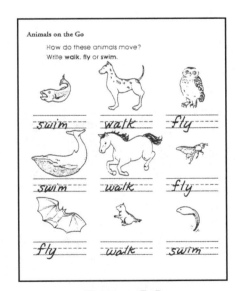

**Animals on the Go**

How do these animals move?
Write **walk**, **fly** or **swim**.

swim    walk    fly
swim    walk    fly
fly     walk    swim

**Page 14**

**Ocean Community**

Many animals make their homes in an ocean community, but some of the animals in this picture do not belong.

Draw an **X** on the animals that do **not** belong.

**Page 15**

**Pond Community**

Many animals make their homes in a pond community, but some of the animals in this picture do not belong.

Draw an **X** on the animals that do **not** belong.

## Page 16

**Grassland Community**

Many animals make their homes in a grassland community, but some of the animals in this picture do not belong.

Draw an **X** on the animals that do **not** belong.

## Page 17

**Forest Community**

Many animals make their homes in a forest community, but some of the animals in this picture do not belong.

Draw an **X** on the animals that do **not** belong.

## Page 18

**Animals at Home**

Did you ever see a fish living in a tree? Of course you didn't! Fish live in the water. Help the animals find their homes.

Cut out each animal.
Paste it on its home.
Color the picture.

robin
bee
squirrel
fish

## Page 19

**The Four Seasons**

1. Cut out and paste the season words on the correct boxes below.

2. Color the clothes for:
   Fall – blue; Winter – red;
   Spring – green; Summer – yellow

Winter    Spring
Summer    Fall

## Page 21

**Pick a Pouch**

Cut and paste each word on the correct kangaroo pouch. Then color one kangaroo green and the other your favorite color.

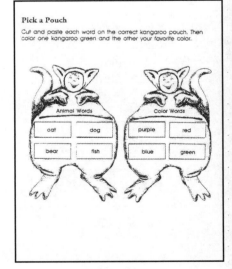

Animal Words

| cat | dog |
| bear | fish |

Color Words

| purple | red |
| blue | green |

## Page 23

**Cake Faces**

Cut and paste the words where they belong.

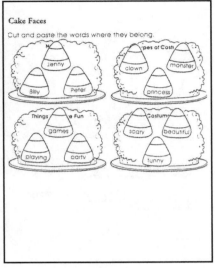

**Page 25**

**What a Trick!**

If the word names an animal, color the space brown.
If the word names something to eat, color the space blue.
If the word names something found in the sky, color the space yellow.
If the word names a piece of furniture, color the space red.
If the word names something you use in school, color the space green.

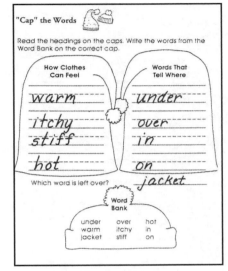

**Page 27**

**"Cap" the Words**

Read the headings on the caps. Write the words from the Word Bank on the correct cap.

| How Clothes Can Feel | Words That Tell Where |
|---|---|
| *warm* | *under* |
| *itchy* | *over* |
| *stiff* | *in* |
| *hot* | *on* |
| | *jacket* |

Which word is left over?

**Word Bank**

| under | over | hot |
|---|---|---|
| warm | itchy | in |
| jacket | stiff | on |

**Page 28**

**Where's My Baby?**

Match the adult animal to the baby animal!

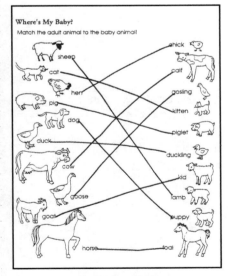

**Page 29**

**Leaf Shapes**

All leaves are not the same. They have different shapes. There are four common shapes.

Draw a line to match the leaf with its shape.

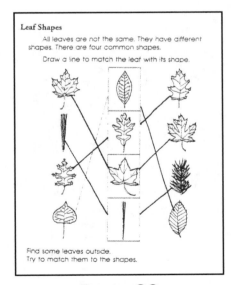

Find some leaves outside.
Try to match them to the shapes.

**Page 30**

**I Slither and Crawl**

Do the puzzle about reptiles.
Color only the reptiles.

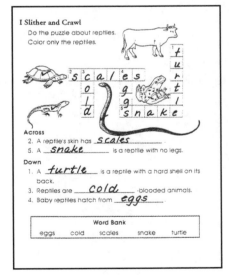

**Across**
2. A reptile's skin has _scales_.
5. A _snake_ is a reptile with no legs.

**Down**
1. A _turtle_ is a reptile with a hard shell on its back.
3. Reptiles are _cold_-blooded animals.
4. Baby reptiles hatch from _eggs_.

| Word Bank | | | | |
|---|---|---|---|---|
| eggs | cold | scales | snake | turtle |

**Page 31**

## A Reptile Riddle

Circle the animal that does not belong in the group. Print the letters beside the circled words in the spaces below to find the answer to the riddle.

**Birds**
1. L robin
   N bluebird
   I (cow)
   J crow

**Insects**
2. L (snake)
   A ladybug
   N wasp
   T bee

**Dogs**
3. B collie
   S beagle
   E shepherd
   L (ox)

**Reptiles**
4. R snake
   I (horse)
   G turtle
   W alligator

**Farm Animals**
5. G (tiger)
   K pig
   O cow
   Y hen

**Jungle Animals**
6. J lion
   B cheetah
   U tiger
   A (rat)

**Zoo Animals**
7. M bear
   O giraffe
   T (dog)
   F zebra

**Ocean Animals**
8. H octopus
   T whale
   K shark
   O (camel)

**Fish**
9. R (raccoon)
   P perch
   V catfish
   L tuna

**Riddle**
'What do you call a sick crocodile?'

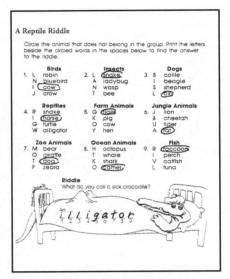

i L L i g a t o r
20 1 2 3 4 5 6 7 8 9

**Page 32**

## I'm Slippery and Cold

Do the puzzle about amphibians.
Color only the amphibians.

**Down**
1. Amphibian babies usually hatch from _eggs_
2. Amphibians are _cold_ -blooded animals.
4. Amphibians often have smooth, moist _skin_

**Across**
3. Amphibian babies breathe with either lungs or _gills_
5. Amphibians live in the water and on _land_

**Word Bank**

land   gills   skin   eggs   cold

**Page 33**

## From Mice to Whales

Do the puzzle about mammals.
Color only the mammals.

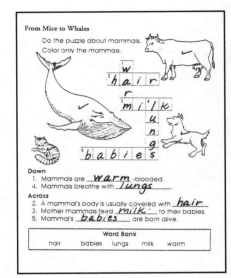

**Down**
1. Mammals are _warm_ -blooded.
4. Mammals breathe with _lungs_

**Across**
2. A mammal's body is usually covered with _hair_
3. Mother mammals feed _milk_ to their babies.
5. Mammal's _babies_ are born alive.

**Word Bank**

hair   babies   lungs   milk   warm

**Page 34**

## Crawling with Insects

Do the puzzle about insects.
Color only the insects.

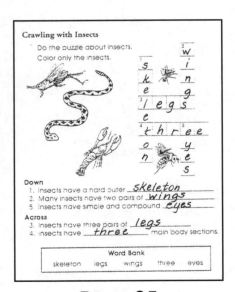

**Down**
1. Insects have a hard outer _skeleton_
2. Many insects have two pairs of _wings_
5. Insects have simple and compound _eyes_

**Across**
3. Insects have three pairs of _legs_
4. Insects have _three_ main body sections.

**Word Bank**

skeleton   legs   wings   three   eyes

**Page 35**

## Fish for Me

Do the puzzle about fish.
Color only the fish.

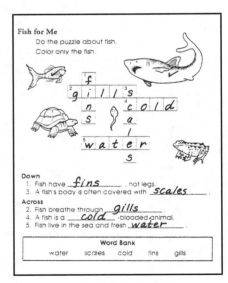

**Down**
1. Fish have _fins_ , not legs.
3. A fish's body is often covered with _scales_

**Across**
2. Fish breathe through _gills_
4. A fish is a _cold_ -blooded animal.
5. Fish live in the sea and fresh _water_

**Word Bank**

water   scales   cold   fins   gills

**Page 36**

## Special People

Use the code to name the special people below.

A C D E F G H I L M O P R T
1 2 3 4 5 6 7 8 9 10 11 12 13 14

POLICE    DOCTOR
OFFICER

FIRE      MAIL
FIGHTER   CARRIER

**Page 37**

## Page 38

My Teacher Helps Me Learn . . .

1. Circle the words from the Word Bank in the puzzle.
2. Then color the circled words green.
3. Last, write your teacher's name on the bottom line.

**Word Bank**
spelling   science   writing   reading   music
art   math   gym   social studies

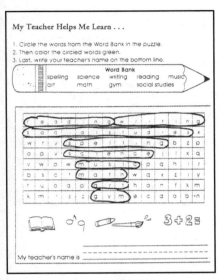

My teacher's name is _____

## Page 39

Explorers of Space

An astronaut is a person who travels in space. Only a few people can become astronauts. They must be in very good health. They must be very smart. There are special schools to train astronauts. Some astronauts are scientists. Some are pilots. They must work hard to be ready to travel in space.

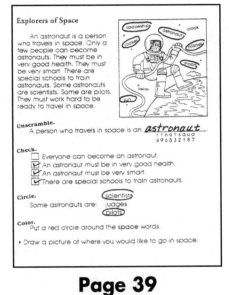

**Unscramble.**
A person who travels in space is an *astronaut*
rtnotsaud
496532187

**Check.**
☐ Everyone can become an astronaut.
☑ An astronaut must be in very good health.
☑ An astronaut must be very smart.
☑ There are special schools to train astronauts.

**Circle.**
Some astronauts are:  (scientists)  judges  (pilots)

**Color.**
Put a red circle around the space words.

• Draw a picture of where you would like to go in space.

## Page 40

Scrambled Continents

Unscramble the words below to spell the continents correctly. Remember to cross out the letters you use. Put in capitals where needed. Use the word bank to help you.

1. rtonn miecara  *North America*
2. ctfara  *Africa*
3. eropeu  *Europe*
4. unots ecaamir  *South America*
5. saia  *Asia*
6. tnrfalacca  *Antarctica*
7. asurilaat  *Australia*

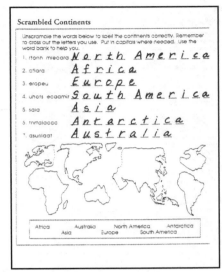

Africa   Australia   North America   Antarctica
Asia   Europe   South America

## Page 41

Alpha-bear-tical Antics

Follow the directions to answer the riddle below. In each paw, print the letter that comes . . .

1. Between H and J   I
2. After G   H
3. Before N   M
4. After A   B
5. Between S and U   T
6. Before S   R
7. After K   L
8. Before B   A
9. Between D and F   E

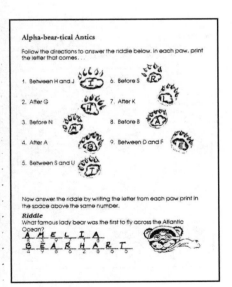

Now answer the riddle by writing the letter from each paw print in the space above the same number.

**Riddle**
What famous lady bear was the first to fly across the Atlantic Ocean?

A M E L I A
B E A R H A R T

## Page 42

Plant Parts

A plant has many parts. Each part has a special job.

**Word Bank**   roots   stem
flower   leaf

Label the parts of the plant.

*flower*
*stem*
*leaf*
*roots*

Draw a line from the plant part to its job.
I make the seeds.
I make food for the plant.
I take water from the roots to the leaves.
I hold the plant in the ground.

Color the roots red.
Color the stem yellow.
Color the leaves green.
Color the flower your favorite color.

green
green
red

## Page 43

Feathered Friends

Name the parts of the bird.

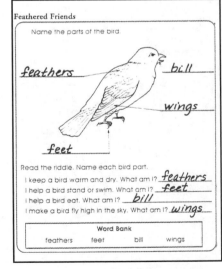

*feathers*   *bill*
*wings*
*feet*

Read the riddle. Name each bird part.
I keep a bird warm and dry. What am I?  *feathers*
I help a bird stand or swim. What am I?  *feet*
I help a bird eat. What am I?  *bill*
I make a bird fly high in the sky. What am I?  *wings*

**Word Bank**
feathers   feet   bill   wings

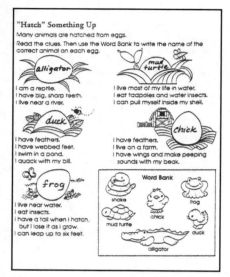

**Page 44**

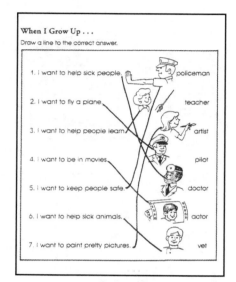

**Page 45**

**Page 48**

**Page 49**

**Page 51**

**Page 52**

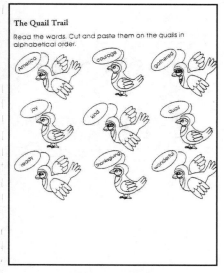

**Page 53**

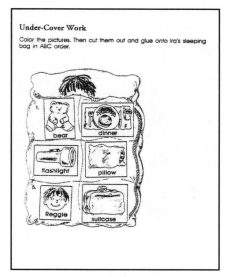

**Page 55**

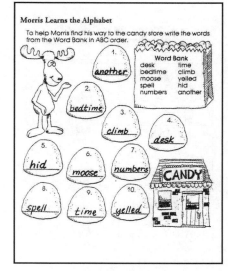

**Page 57**

**Page 58**

**Page 59**

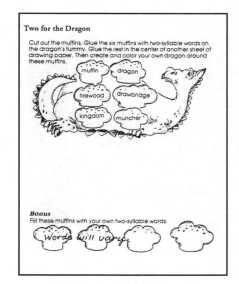

**Page 61**

# Answer Key

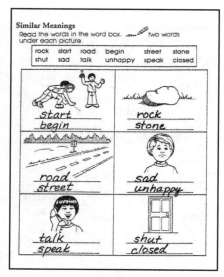

**Similar Meanings**

Read the words in the word box. ✏ two words under each picture.

| rock | start | road | begin | street | stone |
| shut | sad | talk | unhappy | speak | closed |

start
begin

rock
stone

road
street

sad
unhappy

talk
speak

shut
closed

**Page 63**

**Select a Synonym**

Read the words. ✏ the word that means almost the same as the first word.

1. big — cold  loud  (large)
2. yell — (shout)  eat  jump
3. small — good  thin  (little)
4. smile — tall  (grin)  soft
5. boat — talk  (ship)  hop
6. look — (see)  fall  laugh

**Page 64**

**Attach an Antonym**

Read the word on each person. Find the word above the hair that means the opposite and paste it on that head.

hot / cold
play / work
different / same
exciting / boring
dry / wet
out / in
sad / happy
me / you

**Page 65**

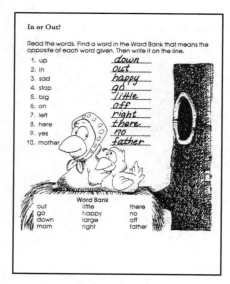

**In or Out?**

Read the words. Find a word in the Word Bank that means the opposite of each word given. Then write it on the line.

1. up — down
2. in — out
3. sad — happy
4. stop — go
5. big — little
6. on — off
7. left — right
8. here — there
9. yes — no
10. mother — father

**Word Bank**

| out | little | there |
| go | happy | no |
| down | large | off |
| mom | right | father |

**Page 67**

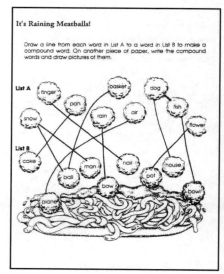

**Two Words in One**

✏ the two words that make up each compound word below.

| snowball | snow | ball |
| raincoat | rain | coat |
| airplane | air | plane |
| watermelon | water | melon |
| haircut | hair | cut |
| football | foot | ball |
| fingernail | finger | nail |
| sunshine | sun | shine |

**Page 68**

**It's Raining Meatballs!**

Draw a line from each word in List A to a word in List B to make a compound word. On another piece of paper, write the compound words and draw pictures of them.

List A: finger, basket, dog, pan, snow, rain, air, fish, flower

List B: cake, man, nail, house, ball, bow, pot, plane, bowl

**Page 69**

230

First Grade Bound © Carson-Dellosa • CD-704634

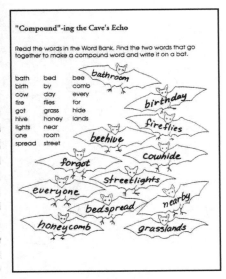

**Page 70**

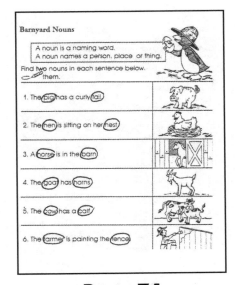

**Page 71**

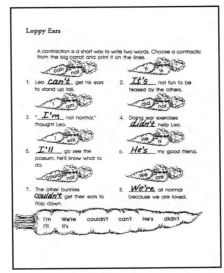

**Page 72**

**Page 73**

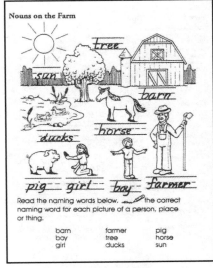

**Page 74**

**Page 75**

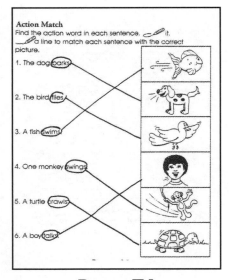

**Page 76**

**Page 77**

**Falling Verbs**

✏ only the leaves that have verbs.

read, rabbit, baby, hops, father, dig, fish, looked, truck, city, jumps, claps, drank, walked

**Page 78**

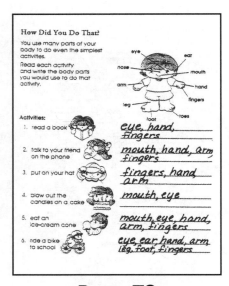

**How Did You Do That?**

You use many parts of your body to do even the simplest activities.

Read each activity and write the body parts you would use to do that activity.

Activities:

1. read a book — *eye, hand, fingers*
2. talk to your friend on the phone — *mouth, hand, arm fingers*
3. put on your hat — *fingers, hand arm*
4. blow out the candles on a cake — *mouth, eye*
5. eat an ice-cream cone — *mouth, eye, hand, arm, fingers*
6. ride a bike to school — *eye, ear, hand, arm leg, foot, fingers*

**Page 79**

**Animal Adjectives**

✏ a describing word in each sentence below. Use the Word Bank to help you.

Word Bank
big, bushy, three, round, green, six

1. A ___ has a *bushy* tail.
2. A ___ has *six* legs.
3. The ___ will become a *green* frog.
4. A ___ has *big* teeth.
5. *Three* ___ hang by their tails.
6. An ___ has *round* eyes.

**Page 80**

**Fishing for Adjectives**

✏ only the fish with describing words.

**Page 81**

## Corn Crackles

Here are some describing words:

sour    furry    sweet    tasty    crisp
tall    crunchy    cloudy    sad    soft

Which four words do you think might best describe the cereal? _____ them on the lines on the cereal box.

crunchy
sweet
tasty
crisp

**Page 82**

## The Turtles Tell

Some sentences tell something.
Telling sentences begin with a capital letter.
Telling sentences end with a period.

_____ only the sentences that tell.

1. Two turtles sat on a log.
2. One turtle fell off.
3. Did you see him?
4. He swam away.
5. The water is cold.
6. Can you swim?

**Page 83**

## All About Dinosaurs

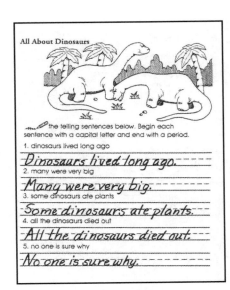

_____ the telling sentences below. Begin each sentence with a capital letter and end with a period.

1. dinosaurs lived long ago

*Dinosaurs lived long ago.*

2. many were very big

*Many were very big.*

3. some dinosaurs ate plants

*Some dinosaurs ate plants.*

4. all the dinosaurs died out

*All the dinosaurs died out.*

5. no one is sure why

*No one is sure why.*

**Page 84**

## State It!

Some sentences tell something. They are called statements. A statement begins with a capital letter and ends with a period.

_____ these statements correctly.

1. jenny planted a seed

*Jenny planted a seed.*

2. she gave it water

*She gave it water.*

3. it sat in the sunshine

*It sat in the sunshine.*

4. the plant began to grow

*The plant began to grow.*

5. leaves grew large

*Leaves grew large.*

6. a flower opened

*A flower opened.*

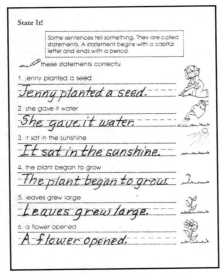

**Page 85**

## Did You Ask Me Something?

Some sentences ask something. They are called questions. A question begins with a capital letter and ends with a question mark.

_____ only the questions.

1. Is that your house?
2. There are two pictures on the wall.
3. Where do you sleep?
4. Do you watch TV in that room?
5. Which coat is yours?
6. The kitten is asleep.

**Page 86**

## Fishy Questions

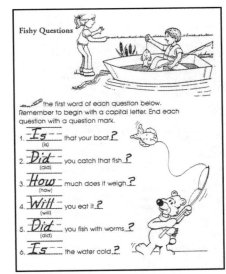

_____ the first word of each question below. Remember to begin with a capital letter. End each question with a question mark.

1. *Is* (is) that your boat?
2. *Did* (did) you catch that fish?
3. *How* (how) much does it weigh?
4. *Will* (will) you eat it?
5. *Did* (did) you fish with worms?
6. *Is* (is) the water cold?

**Page 87**

# Answer Key

## Down on the Farm

A farm is a home for some animals. Horses, cows and pigs live on a farm. Sheep and chickens are farm animals, too. Many farm animals live in a big barn.

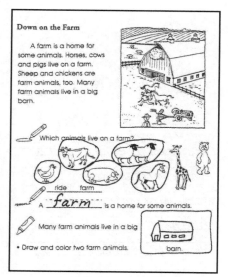

Which animals live on a farm?

ride ~~farm~~

A _farm_ is a home for some animals.

Many farm animals live in a big **barn**.

• Draw and color two farm animals.

**Page 88**

## Pumpkin Patch Pick

Read. Cut and paste each picture where it belongs.

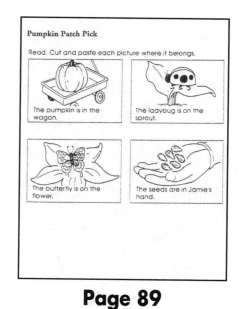

The pumpkin is in the wagon.

The ladybug is on the sprout.

The butterfly is on the flower.

The seeds are in Jamie's hand.

**Page 89**

## My Pet

It is fun to have a pet. Dogs and cats are good pets. Birds and rabbits can be pets, too. Pets are good friends. They need care and love every day.

friends fast

Pets are good _friends_

Pets need care and _love_ long.

dog rabbit cat bird

_dog_      _bird_

_cat_      _rabbit_

**Page 91**

## Mixed-up Colors

Did you know that all colors come from red, yellow or blue? They're the primary colors. Red and blue make purple. Blue and yellow make green. Yellow and red make orange. It is fun to mix paint to make new colors.

**Circle.** Which three colors do you need to make all colors?
red   green   yellow   blue   pink

**Write.** Red, yellow and blue are _primary_ colors.
orange   primary

**Match.**
Red and blue make — orange
Blue and yellow make — purple
Yellow and red make — green

Color the picture: 1 - red     2 - yellow   3 - blue
4 - orange   5 - purple   6 - green

• Draw and color a picture using the primary colors.

**Page 92**

## Just Hanging Around

Bats like to fly at night. They sleep in the daytime. A bat sleeps by hanging upside down. Most bats live in trees and caves. Have you ever seen a bat?

night noon

Bats like to fly at _night_

Bats sleep in the room. daytime

How do bats sleep?

Most bats live in:
☑ trees
☑ caves
☐ floor

the bats black.

• Draw and color a cave with sleeping bats in it.

**Page 93**

## Spinning Spiders

There are many kinds of spiders. Spiders have eight legs. They like to eat insects. Many spiders spin a web. The web is the spider's home. Have you ever seen a spider's web?

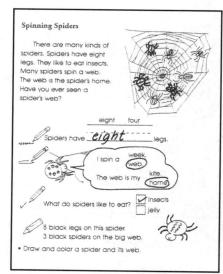

eight four

Spiders have _eight_ legs.

I spin a week. web.

The web is my kite. home.

What do spiders like to eat?
☑ insects
☐ jelly

8 black legs on this spider.
3 black spiders on the big web.

• Draw and color a spider and its web.

**Page 94**

# Answer Key

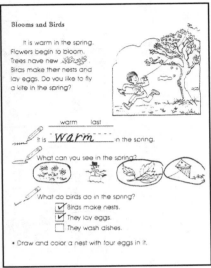

**Blooms and Birds**

It is warm in the spring. Flowers begin to bloom. Trees have new leaves. Birds make their nests and lay eggs. Do you like to fly a kite in the spring?

warm    last

It is **warm** in the spring.

What can you see in the spring?

What do birds do in the spring?
- ☑ Birds make nests.
- ☑ They lay eggs.
- ☐ They wash dishes.

• Draw and color a nest with four eggs in it.

**Page 95**

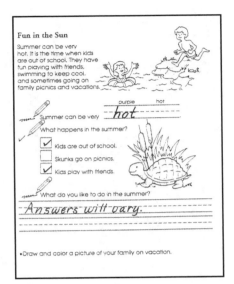

**Fun in the Sun**

Summer can be very hot. It is the time when kids are out of school. They have fun playing with friends, swimming to keep cool, and sometimes going on family picnics and vacations.

purple    hot

Summer can be very **hot**

What happens in the summer?
- ☑ Kids are out of school.
- ☐ Skunks go on picnics.
- ☑ Kids play with friends.

What do you like to do in the summer?

*Answers will vary.*

• Draw and color a picture of your family on vacation.

**Page 96**

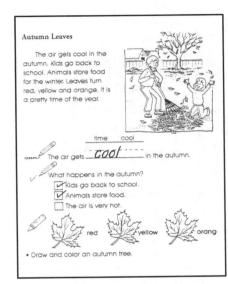

**Autumn Leaves**

The air gets cool in the autumn. Kids go back to school. Animals store food for the winter. Leaves turn red, yellow and orange. It is a pretty time of the year.

time    cool

The air gets **cool** in the autumn.

What happens in the autumn?
- ☑ Kids go back to school.
- ☑ Animals store food.
- ☐ The air is very hot.

red    yellow    orange

• Draw and color an autumn tree.

**Page 97**

**Winter Warm-ups**

Winter can be cold and snowy. Animals stay near each other to keep warm. People wear coats, hats and gloves. Kids can make a snowman. It is fun to play in the snow.

Winter can be:
- ☑ cold
- ☑ snowy
- ☐ purple

like    warm

We try to stay **warm**

What do people wear in the winter?

gloves    hat    pan    coat

a black ___ on the ___.

• Draw and color a snowman.

**Page 98**

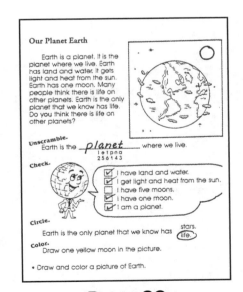

**Our Planet Earth**

Earth is a planet. It is the planet where we live. Earth has land and water. It gets light and heat from the sun. Earth has one moon. Many people think there is life on other planets. Earth is the only planet that we know has life. Do you think there is life on other planets?

Unscramble. Earth is the **planet** where we live.
letpna
256143

Check.
- ☑ I have land and water.
- ☑ I get light and heat from the sun.
- ☐ I have five moons.
- ☑ I have one moon.
- ☑ I am a planet.

Circle. Earth is the only planet that we know has **stars. (life)**

Color. Draw one yellow moon in the picture.

• Draw and color a picture of Earth.

**Page 99**

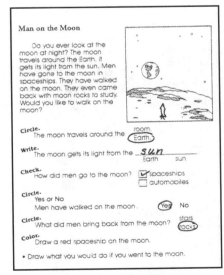

**Man on the Moon**

Do you ever look at the moon at night? The moon travels around the Earth. It gets its light from the sun. Men have gone to the moon in spaceships. They have walked on the moon. They even came back with moon rocks to study. Would you like to walk on the moon?

Circle. The moon travels around the **room. (Earth)**

Write. The moon gets its light from the **sun**    Earth    sun

Check. How did men go to the moon?
- ☑ spaceships
- ☐ automobiles

Circle. Yes or No
Men have walked on the moon. **(Yes)** No

Circle. What did men bring back from the moon? **stars (rocks)**

Color. Draw a red spaceship on the moon.

• Draw what you would do if you went to the moon.

**Page 100**

## A Falling Star

Have you ever seen a falling star? Falling stars are not really stars. They are small pieces of rock. As falling stars fall, they get hot and burn. They look big because they give off so much light. That is why they are so bright in the night sky. Did you know that **meteor** is another name for a falling star?

**Circle.**
Yes or No
A falling star is really a star. — Yes (No)
Falling stars are pieces of rock. — (Yes) No
Falling stars burn as they fall. — (Yes) No

**Check.**
Why does a falling star give off light?
☑ It gets hot and burns.
☐ It has a light bulb in it.

**Unscramble.**
Another name for a falling star is *meteor*
  e r m o t e
  2 6 1 5 3 4

**Color.**
Draw two yellow falling stars in the picture.

• Write a poem about a falling star.

**Page 101**

## Feeling Fantastic!

People can have many feelings. They can be happy. They can be sad. Sometimes people can feel angry. Everyone has feelings.

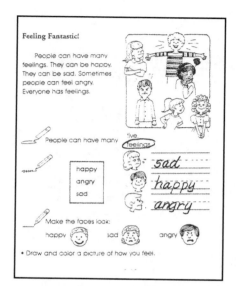

People can have many five (feelings)

happy
angry
sad

*sad*
*happy*
*angry*

Make the faces look:

happy    sad    angry

• Draw and color a picture of how you feel.

**Page 102**

## Fun with Friends

A friend is someone you like very much. Friends play together. Friends help each other, too. It is nice to have many friends.

A *friend* is someone you like.
  friend  from

Yes or No

Friends play together. — (Yes) No
Friends are cars. — Yes (No)
Friends help each other. — (Yes) No

Which are friends?

• Draw and color a picture of you and your friends.

**Page 103**

## In the Cockpit

A pilot is a person who can fly an airplane. A pilot went to a special school to learn to fly a plane. Some pilots fly planes for fun. Some pilots fly planes as their jobs. A pilot sits in a special part of the plane called the **cockpit**. Have you ever seen a pilot sitting in the cockpit of a plane?

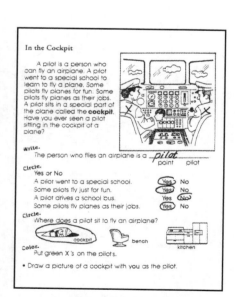

**Write.**
The person who flies an airplane is a *pilot*
  point  pilot

**Circle.**
Yes or No
A pilot went to a special school. — (Yes) No
Some pilots fly just for fun. — (Yes) No
A pilot drives a school bus. — Yes (No)
Some pilots fly planes as their jobs. — (Yes) No

**Circle.**
Where does a pilot sit to fly an airplane?

cockpit    bench    kitchen

**Color.**
Put green X's on the pilots.

• Draw a picture of a cockpit with you as the pilot.

**Page 104**

## On the Farm

Farmers have a very important job. They grow most of the food that we eat. Some farmers grow plants such as oats, corn and wheat. Some farmers raise animals for food. They sell milk from cows. They sell eggs from chickens. Many farmers use machines to help them do their work.

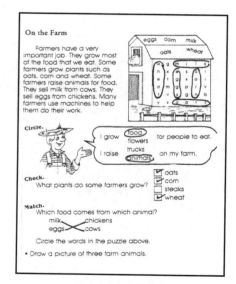

eggs  corn  milk
oats  wheat

**Circle.**
I grow (food) flowers for people to eat.
I raise trucks (animals) on my farm.

**Check.**
What plants do some farmers grow?
☑ oats
☑ corn
☐ steaks
☑ wheat

**Match.**
Which food comes from which animal?
milk ⤬ chickens
eggs ⤬ cows

Circle the words in the puzzle above.

• Draw a picture of three farm animals.

**Page 105**

## We Care for You

Doctors help many people. They help sick people get well. They help healthy people stay well. People go to special schools to learn to be doctors. There are many kinds of doctors. There are doctors for children, eye doctors, ear doctors, bone doctors and heart doctors. Would you like to be a doctor?

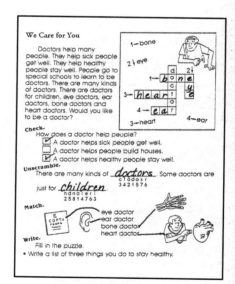

1—bone
2—eye
1—bone
3—heart
4—ear
3—heart
4—ear

**Check.**
How does a doctor help people?
☑ A doctor helps sick people get well.
☐ A doctor helps people build houses.
☑ A doctor helps healthy people stay well.

**Unscramble.**
There are many kinds of *doctors* Some doctors are
  c t o d o s r
  3 4 2 1 5 7 6
just for *children*
  h d n c l e r i
  2 5 8 1 4 7 6 3

**Match.**
eye doctor
ear doctor
bone doctor
heart doctor

**Write.**
Fill in the puzzle.
• Write a list of three things you do to stay healthy.

**Page 106**

# Answer Key

### Animal Homes
Follow the directions below to finish the picture.

1. Draw a fish in the lake.
2. Draw a whale in the ocean.
3. Draw a dog beside the river.
4. Draw a goat on the mountain.
5. Draw a bird on the island.
6. Now color the picture.

**Page 107**

### My Family
1. Color the roof **brown**.
2. Color the chimney **red**.
3. Color the bushes **green**.
4. Draw a picture of your family inside the house.
5. Write your address at the bottom of the page.

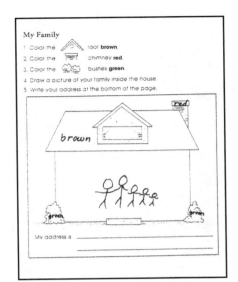

**Page 108**

### Native American Homes
1. Write **tepee** in box 1.
2. Write **adobe** in box 2.
3. Write **wigwam** in box 3.
4. Write **longhouse** in box 4.
5. Draw a sun on the tepee.
6. Color the longhouse **brown**.
7. Draw a door on the wigwam.
8. Draw small windows on the adobe.

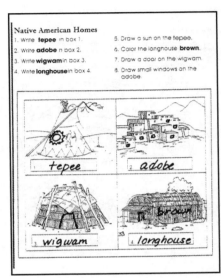

**Page 109**

### Dressed and Ready
1. Draw a picture of you and a friend going to school.
2. Dress you and your friend correctly for the weather.
3. Write your school's name on the sign.

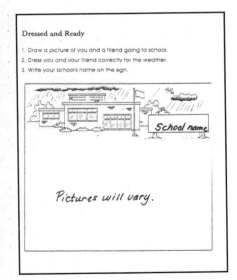

Pictures will vary.

**Page 110**

### Land Ho!
1. Draw a ○ around the word **mountains**. Then color the mountains **black**.
2. Draw a □ around the word **hills**. Then color the hills **green**.
3. Draw a △ around the word **plains**. Then color the plains **brown**.
4. Put an **X** under the word **water**. Then color the water **blue**.

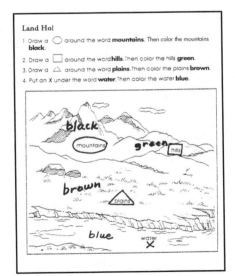

**Page 111**

### Scrambled Shoes
Minnie needs new shoes. She tries on several pairs and decides on one pair. Oops! While trying on all of the shoes, she has scattered them all over. Now she can't find the other shoe of the pair she wants! Help Minnie find her shoe. Using a different color for each pair of shoes, color each pair exactly the same. Then draw a circle around Minnie's missing shoe.

**Page 112**

First Grade Bound © Carson-Dellosa • CD-704634

237

**Barbecue Mishap**

Meg and her family are barbecuing hamburgers. A gust of wind blows the flames toward a tree. Oh no! The tree is on fire! A fire truck races to the fire.

Trace the different ways the firefighters can get to Meg's house.

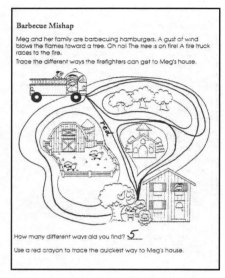

How many different ways did you find? _5_

Use a red crayon to trace the quickest way to Meg's house.

### Page 113

**Musician's Choice**

Many different instruments are used to make music. Irene knows how to play several musical instruments.

Irene knows how to play these instruments.

Irene does not know how to play these instruments.

Draw a circle around the instruments Irene probably also knows how to play.

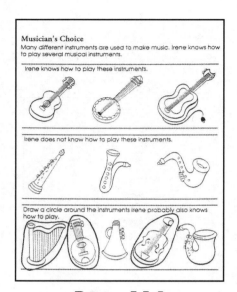

### Page 114

**Family Portraits**

Families may be big or small. No matter how many people are in a family, each person is important to the others.

Cut out the pictures at the bottom of the page. Read the clues. Paste the pictures of the members of this family in the frame where they belong.

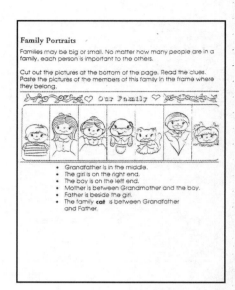

- Grandfather is in the middle.
- The girl is on the right end.
- The boy is on the left end.
- Mother is between Grandmother and the boy.
- Father is beside the girl.
- The family **cat** is between Grandfather and Father.

### Page 115

**Playing Parts**

Look at each picture. Find the title of the story that Grace is acting out in the Word Bank. Write it under the correct picture.

*Space Adventures*

*Cowboy Jake & the Roundup*

*The Lost Treasure Chest*

*The Case of the Missing Cat*

**Word Bank**

The Case of the Missing Cat
Space Adventures

Cowboy Jake & the Roundup
The Lost Treasure Chest

### Page 117

**What Will They Do?**

Read each sentence and question. ✐ a ✓ in the box by the correct answer. ✐ a picture to answer the question.

The boy is putting on his skates.
What will he do?
☐ He will go swimming.
☑ He will go skating.
Draw.

The girl fills her glass with milk.
What will she do?
☑ She will drink the milk.
☐ She will drop the milk.
Draw.

The lady wrote a letter to her friend.
What will she do?
☐ She will throw the letter away.
☑ She will mail the letter.
Draw.

The kids gave Sally a birthday gift.
What will she do?
☑ She will open the gift.
☐ She will not open the gift.
Draw.

### Page 118

**What's the Idea?**

Read the sentence in each speech bubble. Underline the main idea.

My tummy hurts.
The mouse wants more to eat. <u>The mouse ate too much cheese.</u>

My hat is blowing away.
<u>It is a very windy day.</u>
He doesn't want a hat.

I am seven years old today.
The cake is very big.
<u>Today is her birthday.</u>

I can't find my home.
<u>The cat is lost.</u>
The cat has a new home.

May I have more ice cream?
She likes cake best.
<u>She likes ice cream a lot.</u>

### Page 119

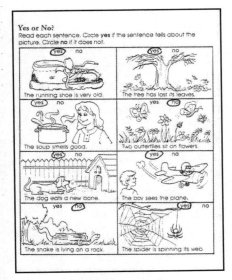

**Page 120**

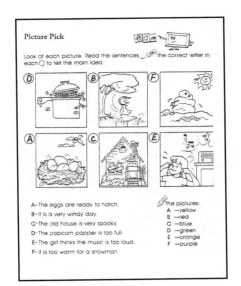

**Page 121**

**Page 122**

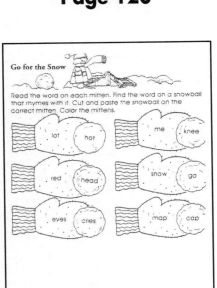

**Page 123**

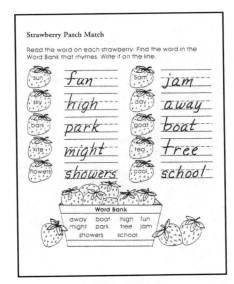

**Page 125**

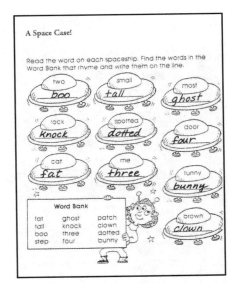

**Page 126**

**Page 127**

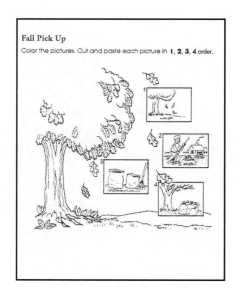

**Page 129**

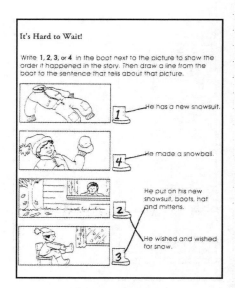

**Page 131**

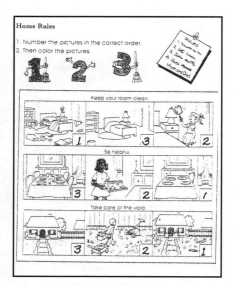

**Page 132**

**Page 133**

**Page 136**

**Page 137**

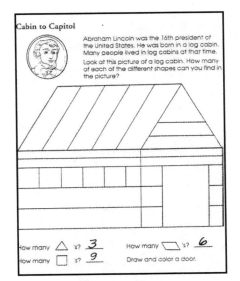

**Page 138**

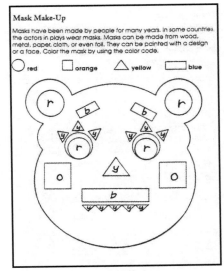

**Page 139**

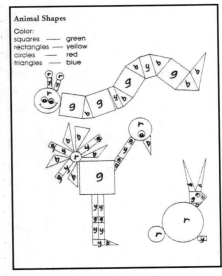

**Page 140**

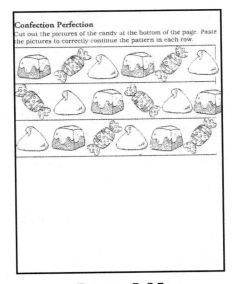

**Page 141**

**Page 143**

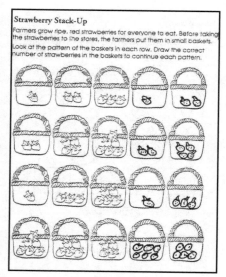

**Page 145**

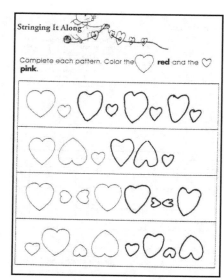

**Page 146**

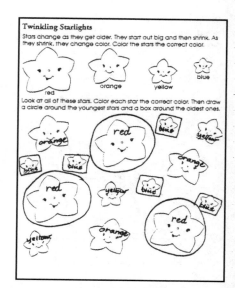

**Page 147**

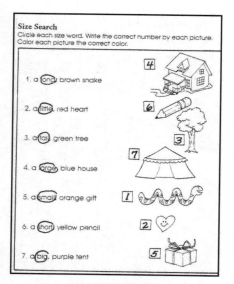

**Page 148**

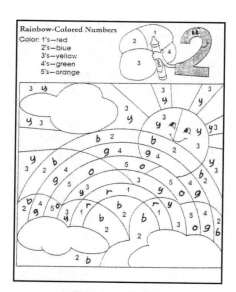

**Page 149**

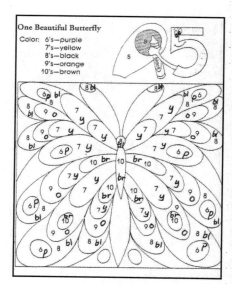

**Page 150**

**Page 151**

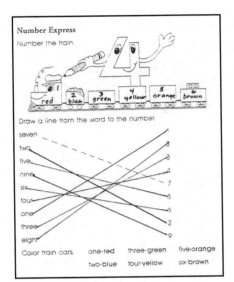

**Page 152**

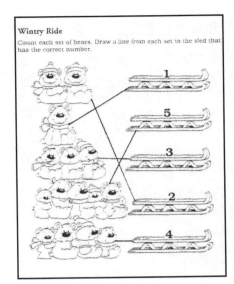

**Page 153**

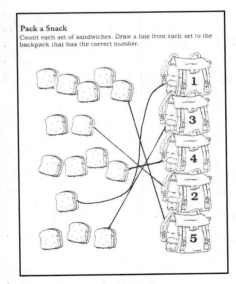

**Page 154**

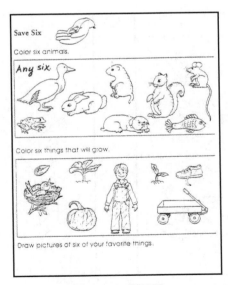

**Page 155**

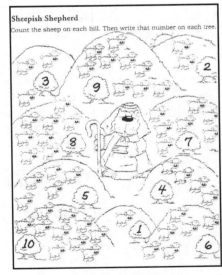

**Page 156**

**Page 157**

**Page 158**

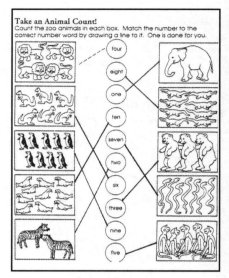

**Page 159**

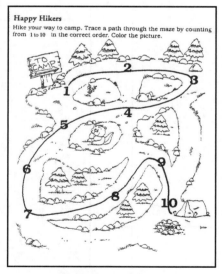

**Page 160**

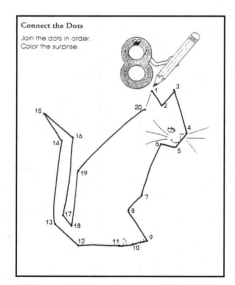

**Page 161**

# Answer Key

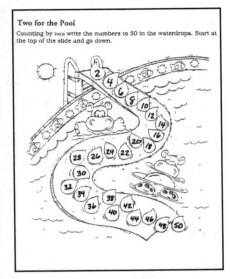

**Page 162**

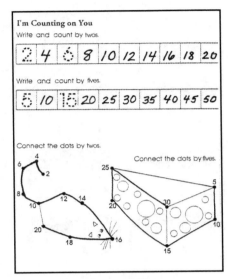

**Page 163**

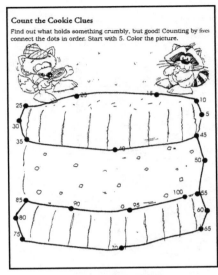

**Page 164**

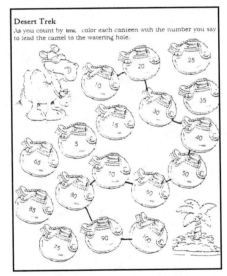

**Page 165**

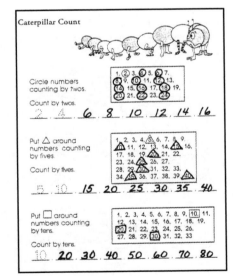

**Page 166**

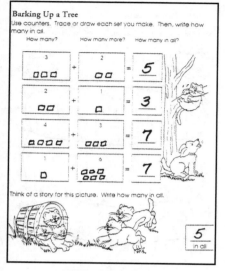

**Barking Up a Tree**
Use counters. Trace or draw each set you make. Then, write how many in all.

How many?    How many more?    How many in all?

3 + 2 = **5**

2 + 1 = **3**

4 + 3 = **7**

1 + 6 = **7**

Think of a story for this picture. Write how many in all.

**5** in all

**Page 167**

**How Many in All?**

2 + 2 = 4

$$\begin{array}{r} 2 \\ + 2 \\ \hline 4 \end{array}$$

Write an addition sentence and a vertical fact for each picture story. Find how many in all.

3 + **1** = 4    $\begin{array}{r} 3 \\ +1 \\ \hline 4 \end{array}$

2 + **3** = 5    $\begin{array}{r} 2 \\ +3 \\ \hline 5 \end{array}$

**4** + **3** = **7**    $\begin{array}{r} 4 \\ +3 \\ \hline 7 \end{array}$

2 + **6** = **8**    $\begin{array}{r} 2 \\ +6 \\ \hline 8 \end{array}$

**5** + 3 = **8**    $\begin{array}{r} 5 \\ +3 \\ \hline 8 \end{array}$

2 + **5** = **7**    $\begin{array}{r} 2 \\ +5 \\ \hline 7 \end{array}$

**Page 168**

**Addition Using Counters**

Example    2 + 1 = **?**

Use counters to add.

Put in 2.    Put in 1 more.
How many counters are there in all? **3**
So, 2 + 1 = **3**. The number that tells how many in all is called the **sum**. The sum of 2 + 1 is 3.

Use counters to find each sum.

2 + 4 = **6**

5 + 2 = **7**

3 + 3 = **6**

3 + 4 = **7**

**Page 169**

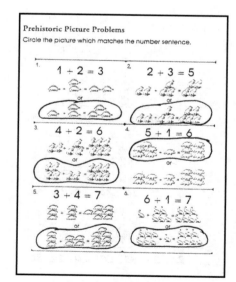

**Prehistoric Picture Problems**
Circle the picture which matches the number sentence.

1. 1 + 2 = 3
2. 2 + 3 = 5
3. 4 + 2 = 6
4. 5 + 1 = 6
5. 3 + 4 = 7
6. 6 + 1 = 7

**Page 170**

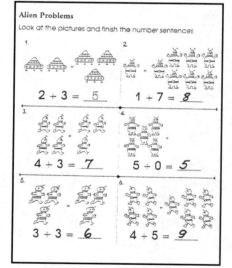

**Alien Problems**
Look at the pictures and finish the number sentences.

1. 2 + 3 = **5**
2. 1 + 7 = **8**
3. 4 + 3 = **7**
4. 5 + 0 = **5**
5. 3 + 3 = **6**
6. 4 + 5 = **9**

**Page 171**

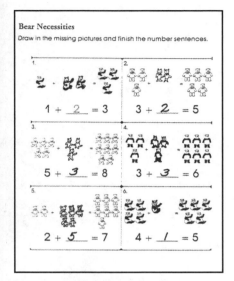

**Page 172**

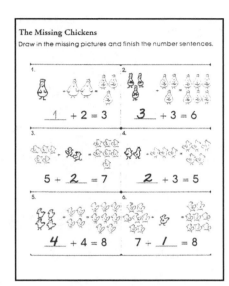

**Page 173**

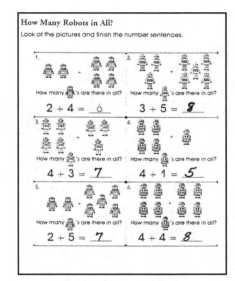

**Page 174**

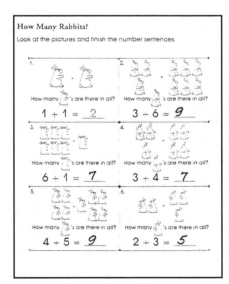

**Page 175**

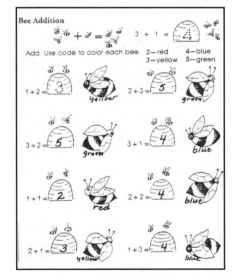

**Page 176**

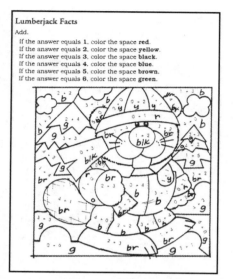

**Page 177**

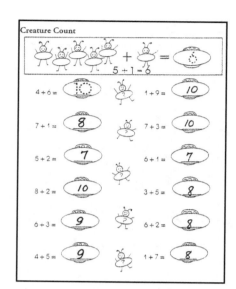

**Page 178**

**Page 179**

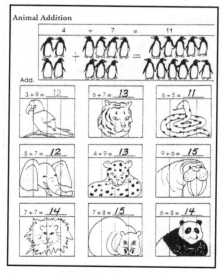

**Page 180**

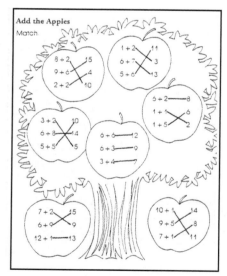

**Page 181**

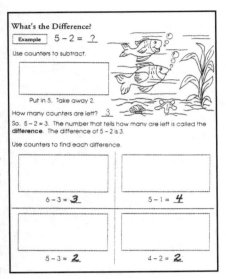

**Page 182**

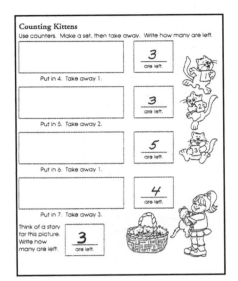

**Page 183**

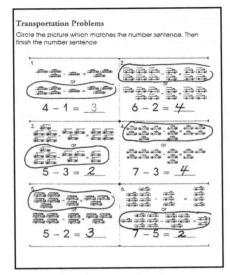

**Page 184**

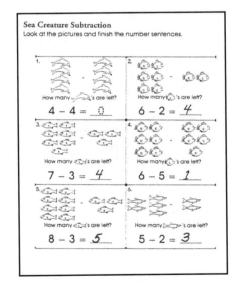

**Page 185**

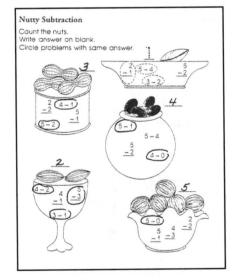

**Page 186**

# Answer Key

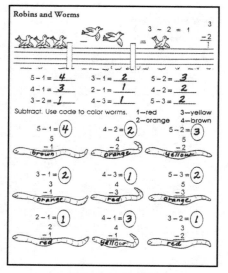

**Page 187**

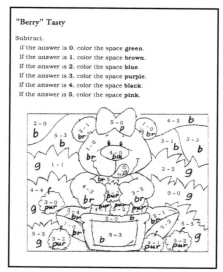

**Page 188**

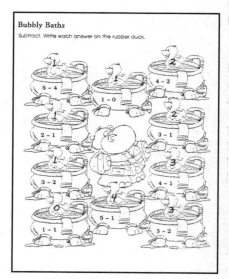

**Page 189**

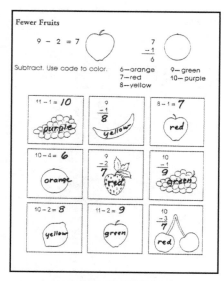

**Page 190**

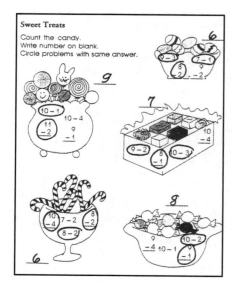

**Page 191**

First Grade Bound © Carson-Dellosa • CD-704634

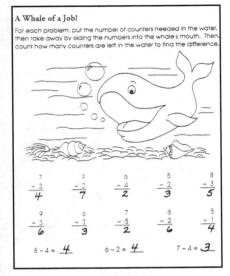

**Page 192**

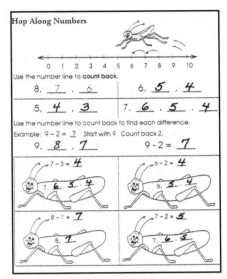

**Page 193**

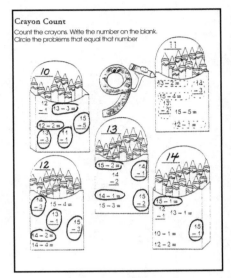

**Page 194**

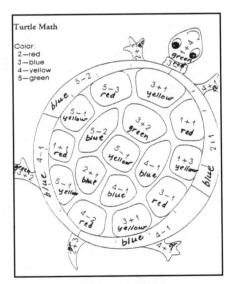

**Page 195**

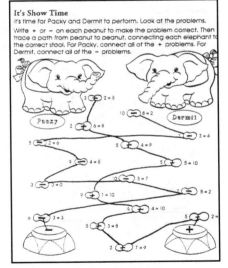

**Page 196**

### Puppy Problems
Look at the pictures and finish the number sentences.

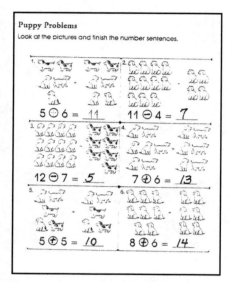

1. $5 \odot 6 = 11$
2. $11 \ominus 4 = 7$
3. $12 \ominus 7 = 5$
4. $7 \oplus 6 = 13$
5. $5 \oplus 5 = 10$
6. $8 \oplus 6 = 14$

**Page 197**

### Calling All Cats
Look at the pictures and finish the number sentences.

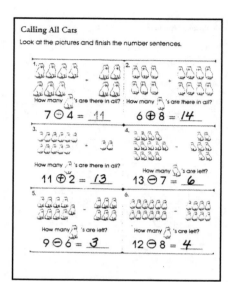

1. How many 's are there in all? $7 \ominus 4 = 11$
2. $6 \oplus 8 = 14$
3. How many 's are there in all? $11 \oplus 2 = 13$
4. How many 's are left? $13 \ominus 7 = 6$
5. How many 's are left? $9 \ominus 6 = 3$
6. How many 's are left? $12 \ominus 8 = 4$

**Page 198**

### What Was the Question?
Draw a line under the question that matches the picture. Then finish the number sentence.

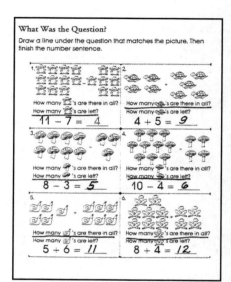

1. How many 's are there in all? How many 's are left? $11 - 7 = 4$
2. How many 's are left? $4 + 5 = 9$
3. How many 's are there in all? How many 's are left? $8 - 3 = 5$
4. How many 's are there in all? How many 's are left? $10 - 4 = 6$
5. How many 's are there in all? How many 's are left? $5 + 6 = 11$
6. How many 's are there in all? How many 's are left? $8 + 4 = 12$

**Page 199**

### Sunny Day Delight
Draw a line under the question that matches the picture. Then finish the number sentence.

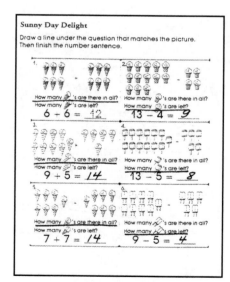

1. How many 's are there in all? How many 's are left? $6 + 6 = 12$
2. How many 's are there in all? How many 's are left? $13 - 4 = 9$
3. How many 's are there in all? How many 's are left? $9 + 5 = 14$
4. How many 's are there in all? How many 's are left? $13 - 5 = 8$
5. How many 's are there in all? How many 's are left? $7 + 7 = 14$
6. How many 's are there in all? How many 's are left? $9 - 5 = 4$

**Page 200**

### Fishing for Answers

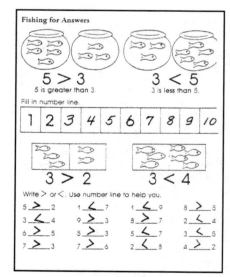

$5 > 3$    5 is greater than 3.
$3 < 5$    3 is less than 5.

Fill in number line.

| 1 | 2 | 3 | 4 | 5 | 6 | 7 | 8 | 9 | 10 |

$3 > 2$      $3 < 4$

Write > or <. Use number line to help you.

5 $>$ 2    1 $<$ 7    1 $<$ 9    8 $>$ 5
3 $<$ 4    9 $>$ 3    8 $>$ 7    2 $<$ 4
6 $>$ 5    5 $>$ 3    5 $<$ 7    3 $<$ 5
7 $>$ 3    7 $>$ 2    2 $<$ 8    4 $<$ 2

**Page 201**

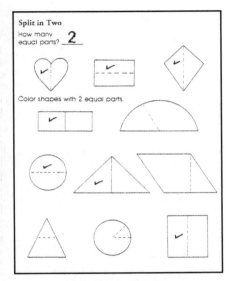

**Page 202**

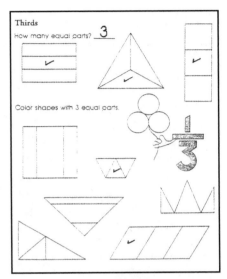

**Page 203**

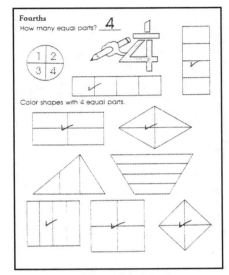

**Page 204**

**Page 205**

**Page 206**

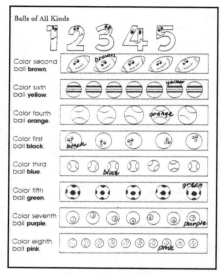

**Page 207**

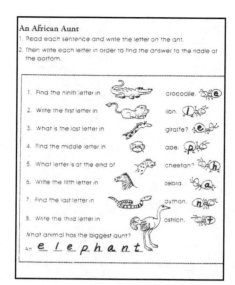

**Page 208**

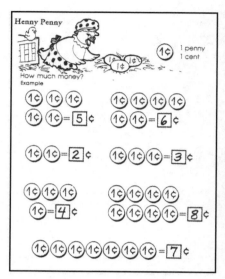

**Page 209**

**Page 210**

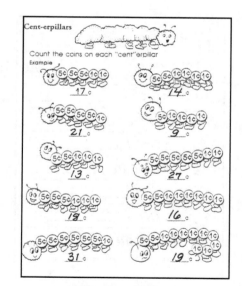

**Page 211**

# Answer Key

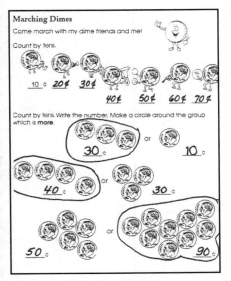

**Marching Dimes**
Come march with my dime friends and me!
Count by tens.

10¢ 20¢ 30¢ 40¢ 50¢ 60¢ 70¢

Count by tens. Write the number. Make a circle around the group which is **more**.

30¢ or 10¢

40¢ or 30¢

50¢ or 90¢

### Page 212

**Buy and Buy**
Circle the coins to equal the right amount.

Example
32¢

26¢

21¢

14¢

54¢

31¢

44¢

42¢

### Page 213

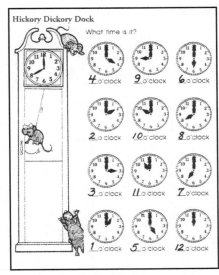

**Hickory Dickory Dock**
What time is it?

4 o'clock   9 o'clock   6 o'clock
2 o'clock   10 o'clock   8 o'clock
3 o'clock   11 o'clock   7 o'clock
1 o'clock   5 o'clock   12 o'clock

### Page 214

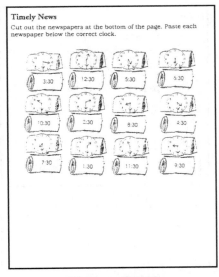

**Timely News**
Cut out the newspapers at the bottom of the page. Paste each newspaper below the correct clock.

3:30   12:30   5:30   6:30
10:30   2:30   8:30   4:30
4   7:30   1:30   11:30   9:30

### Page 215

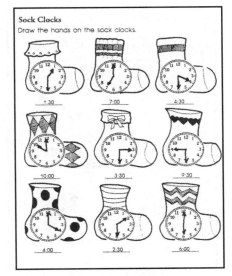

**Sock Clocks**
Draw the hands on the sock clocks.

1:30   7:00   4:30
10:00   3:30   9:30
4:00   2:30   6:00

### Page 217

# Answer Key

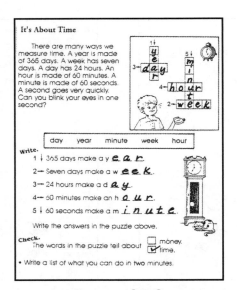

**It's About Time**

There are many ways we measure time. A year is made of 365 days. A week has seven days. A day has 24 hours. An hour is made of 60 minutes. A minute is made of 60 seconds. A second goes very quickly. Can you blink your eyes in one second?

| day | year | minute | week | hour |

Write.

1 ↓ 365 days make a y **e a r**

2→ Seven days make a w **e e k**.

3→ 24 hours make a d **a y**.

4→ 60 minutes make an h **o u r**.

5 ↓ 60 seconds make a m **i n u t e**.

Write the answers in the puzzle above.

Check.
The words in the puzzle tell about ☐ money. ☑ time.

• Write a list of what you can do in two minutes.

**Page 218**

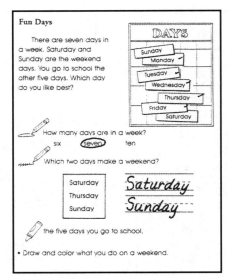

**Fun Days**

There are seven days in a week. Saturday and Sunday are the weekend days. You go to school the other five days. Which day do you like best?

How many days are in a week?
six (seven) ten

Which two days make a weekend?

| Saturday |
| Thursday |
| Sunday |

*Saturday*
*Sunday*

the five days you go to school.

• Draw and color what you do on a weekend.

**Page 219**

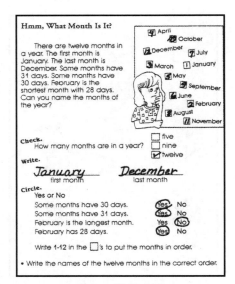

**Hmm, What Month Is It?**

There are twelve months in a year. The first month is January. The last month is December. Some months have 31 days. Some months have 30 days. February is the shortest month with 28 days. Can you name the months of the year?

Check.
How many months are in a year? ☐ five ☐ nine ☑ twelve

Write.

*January*     *December*
first month      last month

Circle.
Yes or No
Some months have 30 days.        (Yes) No
Some months have 31 days.        (Yes) No
February is the longest month.    Yes (No)
February has 28 days.             (Yes) No

Write 1-12 in the ☐'s to put the months in order.

• Write the names of the twelve months in the correct order.

**Page 220**

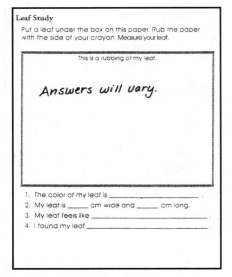

**Leaf Study**

Put a leaf under the box on this paper. Rub the paper with the side of your crayon. Measure your leaf.

This is a rubbing of my leaf.

*Answers will vary.*

1. The color of my leaf is _____.
2. My leaf is _____ cm wide and _____ cm long.
3. My leaf feels like _____
4. I found my leaf _____

**Page 221**

256

First Grade Bound © Carson-Dellosa • CD-704634